PENGUIN BOOKS

BURNING ROSES IN MY GARDEN

T0200887

Celebrating 35 Years of
Penguin Random House India

TASLIMA NASRIN

Edited and Translated by **JESSE WATERS**

PENGUIN BOOKS

An imprint of Penguin Random House

PENGUIN BOOKS

USA | Canada | UK | Ireland | Australia
New Zealand | India | South Africa | China | Singapore

Penguin Books is part of the Penguin Random House group of companies
whose addresses can be found at global.penguinrandomhouse.com

Published by Penguin Random House India Pvt. Ltd
4th Floor, Capital Tower 1, MG Road,
Gurugram 122 002, Haryana, India

First published in Penguin Books by Penguin Random House India 2023

ISBN 9780143449560

Typeset in Monticello LT Pro by Manipal Technologies Limited, Manipal
Printed at Thomson Press India Ltd, New Delhi

www.penguin.co.in

CONTENTS

INTRODUCTION

In the spring of 2010, I had been at Elizabethtown College, Pennsylvania, US, as a visiting assistant professor for approximately two years. But I'd just been told that I would be brought on full-time as director of the Bowers Writers House, a new interdisciplinary venue which I had helped design for the college, and that I would become the chair of the Woodrow Wilson Visiting Fellow committee on our campus. As you probably know, this is a programme sponsored by the Council of Independent Colleges, and enables smaller, private liberal arts colleges to bring amazing world-renowned scholars, politicians, artists and other personalities akin to the liberal arts experience to their respective campuses. That autumn of 2010 I'd been told our visiting fellow would be someone named Naslima Tasrin, a woman with a fascinating past and an amazing catalogue of experiences across the globe. But no matter how much I researched initially, I couldn't find anyone by that name— until one of my colleagues set me straight: our visiting fellow was named Taslima Nasrin, not Naslima Tasrin. I smiled for a moment at the apparent interchangeability of those first letters, a certain malapropism I'll address in just a moment.

So, on a mid-Monday morning in the middle of September, I found myself waiting at the train station just a few miles from our college in anticipation of the week's worth of activities Dr Nasrin would spend with us. I had arranged classes for her to visit, meals with faculty and staff, student groups with which she could engage, and two campus-wide events open to the community: one, a reading of her poetry, the other a discussion of her life's work fighting for those who have neither voice nor champion.

I was proud of the schedule I had built for her. Our campus communities would have a rich set of engagements with someone involved in the kind of work, writing and life force that amplifies our college's mission of 'Educate for service'. And after a bit of investigation, I'd found a community of Indian and Bangladeshi expatriates living in Lancaster (about 20 miles from our college) who were very excited about Dr Nasrin's visit to our community, a group of about fifteen men and women for whom I had arranged a dinner with our guest. I walked to the platform and helped my guest gather her bags, and as the rest of the departing travellers made their way to wherever it was they were going, we briefly introduced ourselves to one another as we walked to my car.

'I think you'll be excited,' I told my guest as we were about to reach my vehicle. 'I've organized a dinner with some folks in Lancaster from India and Bangladesh who are excited to meet you.'

Dr Nasrin stopped in her tracks and gave me a look I will never forget: 'Why did you do that?' she asked softly but insistently, and intently. Reading this, one might ask themselves why a simple invitation to dinner would be met with such a reaction, but when the greater part of your life has been spent hearing cries of the fatwa from the streets below your apartment, hundreds of thousands of people all over the world literally marching in the street demanding your execution, it can be difficult to find even the smallest moment of tranquillity.

Taslima Nasrin. Naslima Tasrin. What does it mean to create a new identity for yourself, to reinvent yourself because of a need you see in the world? What does it mean to feel as if going back to the person you were before would kill you . . . and yet the life you've chosen could mean that very same thing for you each waking day?

To truly understand the voice behind the poems collected in this book, we have to understand what it means to both desire a new self and to be forced by your community to then reject that self, we must prepare ourselves to look into the heart and soul of a woman brilliant enough to know what she is capable of, yet compassionate enough to offer it to the world. A person under these kinds of duress—personal, political, familial, romantic—needs to be a chameleon, a master of voices and appearances, a person who can speak equally to kings, clan leaders and kinfolk. That person is my friend, the incomparable Dr Taslima Nasrin.

Burning Roses in My Garden is an apt title for this collection. Whether we're reading about a woman losing her mother or walking down the streets of her hometown as a young person witnessing the strange and, at times, monstrous differences in the way men and women are treated, and treat one another, we'll find within these pages a voice breaking free, or just about to. Dr Nasrin's experiences, intelligence, sensitivities and global vision are all presented here in these poems with equity and precision. The voice here demonstrates experiences, actions and engagements which reveal bravery and individuality, yes, but also loss. And who among us hasn't been in these places, who of us hasn't wondered if the path we have chosen is truly the one we should be walking? All of us have seen both sun and rain, gain and subtraction. And what victories and losses are here! Within these pages, you will feel as if you are intoxicated with the same loves, curious about and, at times, frustrated with the same cultures, broken in these same hearts, and willing to step into a challenging future. In translating these poems, I have attempted to stay as true to that vision as possible, refusing to embellish or change ideas for the sacrifice of rhetoric. If I have added the occasional image or included any poetic perspective here, it is only to amplify the voice of the author, whose work and person I have known for twelve years.

This book is special not only because it has collected here the poems of one of the most significant global female figures of the early twenty-first century, but also because of the way it presents those poems. From memory to impassioned plea to precise and determined explorations of gender and socio-religious issues all the way to intimate sexual identity and what terrorism truly looks like, this collection presents a stunning and perhaps perfect reflection of exactly what the world needs today: a powerful voice irrespective of gender that can cogently and personally examine the most important issues concerning mankind today. Call her Taslima, call her Dr Nasrin, call her woman-warrior—no matter the title given, her poems are a voice the world needs *right now*.

Jesse Waters

VENGEANCE

I picked up a Nobody off the road, a Nobody, and sharing
    random stories
Slept with Nobody.
He was in my bed the whole night,
His chest swollen with pride.
My feet did not touch the ground, my skin quaked—
My lips were pearls, breasts diamonds, my vagina the gate
    to Heaven—
That is how he touched me.
The Nobody did not sleep the entire night. Nobody gave me
All that I wanted and more.

You left promising you'd be back, promising you'd be back
Tomorrow or the day after,
With just a kiss, a dry kiss on the lips in the middle of
    the night.
Leaving behind a body wracked with thirst, set adrift,
You never returned, it's been three months, or is it four?

Who doesn't want more time?
Why did I think you were good for so long?
I wish I could return to that time, that time when I
    thought you were good.

1

If I could get it back, I would give it to the man from the
      road, the Nobody
So much better than you . . . perhaps because you
Were not from the road.

When the man from the street touched me—
Kissed me from head to toe,
From shoulder to shoulder,
His kiss and his storied swim
Did not bring me pleasure.

The only thing that meant knowing
Was knowing it wasn't your kiss,
That the hands touching me were not your hands,
      that you
Would never swim in the lakes of heaven.
That is pleasure.

THE LAST KISS

Let's assume the girl was Girl and the boy was Boy.
That time when Boy came out of nowhere and
    kissed her suddenly,
Kissed the surprised and petrified Girl,
Without love, without a 'See you tomorrow!' or
    'Day after then!'
That time when he kissed her deeply, shattering her
    into fragments,
Broke her, tore her down
In a room swimming with light,
That time when he abruptly and breathlessly kissed her,
Since then, Boy is nowhere to be found.

Girl doesn't know who he was, or where he was from,
She had only seen his eyes, the two shiny marbles in them
Like a pair of those from childhood games,
It's been years since youth was in such a rush,
Never was there ever such a restless breeze in
    someone's gaze . . .
'Was it him?' the girl cried out in sudden surprise.
Then she kept saying to herself,
'Wasn't it him who used to bring her a spinning top
    every day?'

3

As long it would spin, it would seem her palms held the
    entire world.
Her body would tremble as he looked at her
    with amazement,
His eyes would sparkle with the light
Shining off the marbles on the playground,
His stunned eyes were like marbles too.

Was Boy then that boy from the playground,
This Boy who had kissed her?
He who used to bring her the spinning top,
Was he the one who had kissed her all of a sudden?
She did not know if he would return again,
If he would kiss her again.
She did not know he had kissed her
Because there had been no one else to kiss that night,
So, on that stormy night, that quiet night, without a
    second thought,
He had kissed whoever he had found at hand.
The next day, once the high was gone,
He had forgotten all about it as well.

Girl's husband returned over the weekend
To perform his marital duties,
But when her husband tried to kiss her,
She turned her face and lips away,

4

I give you my body, ravage me all day if you will,
All night, taste me from head to toe,
Just don't kiss me.

She keeps the memories of that last kiss alive.
The kiss that brought an entire world within her grasp,
The kiss that brought her a rush of youth,
His kiss was becoming more than him,
Her youth was becoming more than the kiss—
The dream of youth bigger than youth itself.
The dreams were so bright they made the marble-eyed boy
    grow dim—
His nightly addiction, his willingness to kiss whoever—
His forgetting, and not returning.

A RESPECTABLE NOTICE

Listen, O Man!
Hold on a moment. Wait.
Wait and listen to my final words, I don't want you,
I don't want *you*, no, I don't *want* you.
Your eyes . . . your voice, that skin, all of these are
No quality. Whatever you speak is a lie.
That you love me is not reason enough to want you,
There are many who love me so much more beautifully
    than you . . .
And they lie a lot less.

If you think I want you because the way you touch me
Is how I want to be touched—
If you think I want you because the way you lead me into
    the dark
Is how I want someone to lead me—
If you think I want you because you make me lose myself
In the chaos of my own body, and believe yourself this
Is how I want to lose myself, you are wrong.
This is a careful notice. This is my coda.
I can glibly ask you to leave, shut the door behind you
And not open it for as long as you are alive.

You are the heir brought up on milk and honey,
The Lord who thought his manhood the only treasure.
You thought I would swoon, worship that worm.
You thought I could not do without your treasure
Or your pity . . . an organ tiny as tongues of greed.

But the worm, the armless buzzing I truly fear and hate
Is not the puny slug between your legs
But the oozing snake alive inside the head,
Growing bigger even than that head in your five-foot-
        something frame—
Watered and nourished by the silence: your relatives, your
        friends, your
Neighbours, your colleagues, your lovers and your wives—

As far as your eyes can see, look! They all stand holding
        water and manure for you.
I will uproot that vestigial organ, now best fit for the
        garbage, and chop
Chop it into pieces for the ragged river fish, and toss them
        into the water . . .

This is my notice. My coda. The dismissal of your rage
That doesn't know your true pride rests in the bigger one.
When you lunge at me, it's not you
But your invisible, huge manhood that lunges,

And when you leave me, it's not you but that organ
    which leaves

And still you return! You push me to kiss your
    worthless worm,
But it's not you—a larger organ, a terrible ghost, insists
When you grab my hair, my breasts, my face,
When you do what you wish with me—
It's not you but an excuse for manhood that does it.
I lie back unsatisfied. This is my notice.
And when you cum in me and leave,
It's not you which is left here . . . but your bigger
    manhood leaves.
Your face is changing, your nose and ears are melting.
You can no longer smell or hear me.
You cannot see me.
Your body is no longer your own.
What you have become is manhood.
Every day a lumbering, pointless manhood

Judging women on a scale, stripping them naked,
Covering them with a burqa. It's what makes women
    into whores,
Leads men to the whorehouses. This pointless manhood?
It spits at women, demands dowries, beats wives,
    sets them aflame.

8

It rapes and murders in the name of something ancient
    but rotten.

I nail this notice to my heart's dark door.
Whether I open my door to the world or not,
If you ever dare to come and stand before it
Leave those horrible worms, those slugs in your head
For the dead. If in you they still live, I—we—don't
    want you.

FOR A NON-LOVER

This is the city you will live in. Running here and there
    for work,
Wandering through the streets where the wet walls touch
    your shoulders
on each side, where no one tells the name of the things
    that are real,
You will drink, slap friends on the back with a laughter
    birds envy.
The world is letting the night doze off . . . but not you.
Some evenings you will visit certain households,
For food, or play, or who knows what—
To nimbly undrape someone's pink sari, peacocks sewn
Down each side—in a house right past my yard.
Perhaps you will walk past this very neighbourhood each day,
Always within reach. Sometimes you will laugh,
    letting me know
That you *are*, and I will curl up, tear myself to shreds.
'I'm too busy these days,' you will laugh, 'I don't
Have the time.' I will save myself
From your non-love. You and I will not see each other,

Years will pass, and by and by, I will forget how
    meeting you—

What colour shirt you used to wear.
How you looked when you laughed.
How you picked your nails while speaking, if it was my eyes
You looked at or somewhere else, how you would shake
Your leg, rise from your chair to draw a glass of water—
I would forget it all, even shake from my mind
Where exactly on your face the freckles were.
I would keep forgetting how it felt kissing you,
How it was to have your face tangled in my hair or my heart.

More years will pass, and you and I will not meet.
In the same city, always, yet we will never lose our way
Back towards each other. We will come across illness
But not each other. Not at some crossroads, nor at a
        petrol pump,
A fish market, the book fair, in restaurants . . . nowhere.

I have decided: when the evening will infiltrate
My silent room with a flash of light, when my pink sari
Billows in the wild summer storm on the terrace
        and the peacocks
Scream, when I finally spend the night talking to the
        moon and the sky,
That next day, I will tell you: 'Nothing happens if we
        don't truly meet.'
We have not met in one-thousand thousand years.

Does that mean I was not alive? Of course I was!
My desires had drawn you, made you my lover.
My desire has now made you my non-lover . . .
And I can live out a million years without touching you!

Never think of me as alone, your non-love stays by my side.
The peacocks are screaming. My heart is a Goddess-tail of
     perfect colours.

A BOUQUET OF SCARLET ENVY

When you used to say you were not into anyone,
    I felt good.
You *had* said you were old, you didn't care for it any more—
You know, sex, etc.
I had brushed it aside: 'There's hardly a wrinkle
    on your skin!'
I hoped I'd mapped you out: from your office, then
    catching up
With friends in the evening, alcohol, then reading
Poetry on stage. Not chasing purple skirts, not trying to
    lure them to bed . . .
I took it seriously when you said you were old,
That you had carefully tucked away all your unsteady bits,
That, perhaps, on certain afternoons, I'm a raging storm
You were lost in once, drowning—
The very reason why your tastes have run so dry.
After all, sex—desired or not—was always within
    your grasp.
Those purple skirts, pink sari . . . were you a rapist
Who now has washed their hands of desire?
Are you leaving this up to God?
And so . . . matted and scarlet, I had thought you were
    fumbling

Your way back home at dusk.

Perhaps you *were* on your way back,
But while with me, you used to roll around 'til late,
Now a different body fills that role.
You told me yourself, after years, away
So long that you forgot the truth
Was always the lie. But now awake, you sleep,
You forget the time, such a wild, wet time in the rain
When we would swim in each other as if we were young.
And the hundred poems I wrote for you! The ones you read!
So beautiful in the dark clouds rumbling in your voice
     over my head!
All forgotten . . . and because you don't remember
The pursuit of the housewives with whom you slept
At every chance in these households, in the lanes and by-
     lanes of this city,
Nothing in the storm will ever be the same: 'I bet you
     always wanted to be

Casanova,' I might say to you. 'No, no,' you'd lie.
Lying used to look good on you. Believing
In you looked good on me. 'I'm with a new one now,'
You smiled. 'And you,' you asked, 'Who are you
With now?'
'No one.'

'No one?'
I mapped you again, scarlet in the wind of my throat,
    'Didn't you
Tell me you were old? That you weren't into sex any more!'
'I am not that old.'
'Do you love the girl, the one you're with?'
'Yes, a bit of course.'
Those purple skirts, pink saris, little blue pills . . .
You have lived the safe life of a small-time Casanova in a
    small-time city
And a luck that would make the real Casanova writhe
    in envy.
Our streets, where one will rough you up or say, 'Skip
    town, bastard!'

Not that I have been chaste all these years . . .
Perhaps there's been some love, once or twice—
All I wanted to do today was lie to you,
To tell you that I too was doing well!
'I've got a new love now, great sex, and he's a good,
    sweet man,'
But all I could do was tear to pieces
Those hundred poems, my only lies, now dirt and mud in
    the lake of rain.
I want to swim again in wild weather.
I want to never walk the lane of lies again,

15

But after so many years, I have made myself believe
That none of those hundred poems were for you, not a
  single word.
I douse the poems in that muddy lake, and swing my own
  scarlet skirts
Back to my body and demolish the secret pride you felt
  over them.
As long as you live, I hope you answer every cuckoo
  that calls.

IF YOU REMEMBER, FREEDOM

If you must forget, then do what you must. Go.
Don't pester me with texts and emails, your electronic
Pokes. Hurl that icy silence, and don't bother me so.

If you forget, at least I will know, at least
I will remove these biting shoes, walk barefoot and lose
These waiting garbs, take a shower, and play
The old songs again. If you forget I will throw
all the windows open, and sleep with the moon
Playing hide-and-seek on my body—
Someone thinking of me, wanting me, all of me.
And I would stand in front of them . . . hair, face,
        eyes, lips,

Breasts, chin, thighs, terrifying and perfect.

Not a scratch, tear, or any sign of grime.
There was a time I would have to smile
If the sun was hungry, or wanted tea, terrifying
To me to be perfect—everything!
To love flawlessly!
To immerse myself flawlessly!
To reduce myself flawlessly!

17

I have sewn myself a silk chain of nightmares,
    have become
A slave in your heart, in that trap within your fist.
    Forget me,
So, I can wipe the paint off my face and become light.

RELATIONSHIP WITH A CAT

Cats make for better relatives.
Humans rob and leave, but not cats.
They will wait in the yard—until you
Return they wait. If you blindfold them, leave
Them past the river, they will sniff their way back to you.
Relatives are not the same. When I opened my eyes
    after birth
I was met with a crowd of them. Whiskers, breasts, eyes,
Pawing at my newness . . . I never chose who I wanted
    as relatives.

Cats want nothing other than certainty.
Two square meals a day and water, a corner
Or bed for restful sleep, another corner somewhere
To answer nature's call. A quiet, peaceful house.
Warmth in winter and a cool breeze in summer.
Who doesn't desire restfulness? But now

It's a difficult time. My aunts, cousins, uncles
And nieces have gone one after another as does dust
Behind my blue sari. Year after year. Forgetting bit
By bit each day, they have left for better things.
Amidst this there was a cat.

Cats leave too, they know how.
But once they are your kin
They are not as cruel.
A life lived like this makes family familiar.

Getting to know this cat, sitting with her on our lazy
Balcony in the late afternoon sun, or playing
In the dark of morning, cuddling at night

If all the relatives I have left, if they gather on one side,
The cat on the other,
It is to her that I will go.
In the swell of loneliness, creature is creature,
Friends are friends.
Cats are everything, roaming the neighbourhood,
Declaring their affections in that way cats
Tiptoe, away from prying eyes, that feline way
They love and gather close . . .

I want it, and so do you.
A cat matched to each one of us.
Like the cats we are in secret,
Humanoid cats, big and small.

ON LOVE

You said you loved and disappeared one day.
As if you knew your savings account—my heart—
Would swell and grow and sharpen after a year
Of not seeing or touching my body.

You had thought love would be as you had left it,
No matter what else erodes over time, over bodies,
Love won't, that love could not die or wither
Or else it would not be love!

Love is a knife that can slice through the heart.
It's not as if you don't know that.
Leave it be and you will see it rust
And go blunt. The bread you have baked
Fresh is even tougher than the blade.
If love is a knife, why shouldn't it behave like one?

You can say you love and then go away—
Stay for as many months, years as you wish,
Then cash in your investment.
But if you come back suddenly

You can ask for anything, with interest too—
But do not ask for love.
Ply your trade elsewhere. I don't pawn
My heart, won't let my love come loose.

2.

I am not supposed to lose sleep thinking about him,
Or overlook my day's toil
And sit lost in his thoughts.

He is happy in his own way, somewhere.
This thought distracts me,
And makes me want him, like before,
And makes me wait, even when I'm not meant to.
Living with his tricks, his cunning eyes, his unfaithful
    body, the incessant lies,
Living his heartless, dissolute life—
No one but me will live for this life, for this long.

But I want him so! Because except my own life
I have no one else to play such games with.
In solitude, the investment just sits. I want

Him not because I love him.

Not because I love him, or because my life is empty,
I want him because I want to make him happy.
I want to pour out the last droplet of my perseverance
And make him happy.
I want to give all that I have, every last bit,
And want his nothingness in return.

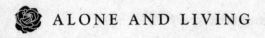 ALONE AND LIVING

Living alone has become a habit.
Removing myself nonchalantly from the crowd
    and being alone.
I have lived with cats for so long—when I see one
It makes me want more cats. They say lonely

Women keep cats, that you will always find
A white, black, ash or golden one
In their homes, maybe a couple.
Whether they cuddle or show affection, or not,
They remain in a corner or somewhere
In the yard. They say women, as they trip
Over hurdles, slip in the mud or water—
As they get burned here and there and there—
Have learnt that keeping cats is still
Better than keeping a man.

Have I not, having kept a man for years, learnt that it's
    like raising a snake?
So many animals on this earth, why keep a man of all things?

I want a creature that listens, understands,
Communicates through glances,

24

Comes close, loves, sleeps beside you
But doesn't scratch or bite. Doesn't draw blood.
Why not keep a pet that brings a lot less trouble?

(IN)DIFFERENCE

I know this pain. Since you entered
My life—and left it—it's familiar to me.
How deep the teeth, the nails of it can go
Into the flesh, the bone's marrow.
In some corner of her heart, you must be thinking, a
    healed wound is waiting
For its chance. You naïve boy!
It's not a kind of pain
I am a stranger to, this landscape—
How much moisture it can drain can't compare to what's
    left behind.
Anybody can give such pain, any boy could leave
Only some sandy surface somewhere near my heart.
Why didn't you offer pain of a different kind?
How immaculately the man-mind can play games . . . you
    were not

Just any boy after all! To you I revealed the sun's blood—
You were different, and the way
I loved you was different.

26

HOW BEAUTIFUL THE MOON IS

If nobody will come for me,
Nobody will call out to me from inside the house,
Nobody will come to put a hand on my shoulder—
If nobody will say, softly, 'See how beautiful the moon
    is tonight
Against your face', I will know my place: in the shrubs
    and bushes.
Behind the door. On the roof, in the dark lanes
    at the crossroads
Where Death waits for what's about to be handed down.
And why not today!
When I stand on the veranda alone—

If everything that is there has to be handed down to death—
Then why not today?
Let Death come today,
Let my unruly living-in with emptiness end today itself.

IF YOU WANT TO LEAVE

If you want to leave, leave exactly the way you stayed—
So smoothly that I don't get even a hint.
Go with the door half ajar, knowing
I will never bolt it from inside.

Go, if you have to go—with two, four pieces of clothing
Forgotten on the stand. In the bathroom leave behind
Your towel, a pair
Of slippers—this way.

The sudden wind also knocks on the door, at times,
On certain nights. I will take it that you had come
And gone because I was sleeping, because I was, to
     you, dead.

BIRTHDAY BLUES

One more step moved forward, another house,
　　another veranda.
To move towards death, life embraces more of land
　　and water—
More acquisitions the length and breadth of affections
　　and affectations.
If we could only stretch them further.
We love to cling to the pain of separation.
We love to cling to the pain of union.

Gift me the flowers of love any other day,
Not on my birthday.
That day the fragrance of flowers makes me
Feel as if I am my own
Expansive tomb.

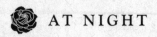 AT NIGHT

She comes down silently, as if from the moon, to stand on
    the sky-veranda—
Walks in sullen indifference as the dark breeds around her—
Sheds the clothing and bathes in the nearby pond.
Her wet hair, spread on the cold rocks of the stone
    sitting wall
Cannot fully dry. Sitting on the bank, she calls for someone
In a broken voice . . . who knows whom!

Afterwards, when no one answers, she descends
    downwards on the
Thin wings of a black cloud.

When the people of the earth
Drift towards sleep, she sighs, and hangs from the old
    Semal tree—
An unknown fragrance comes floating from her body
That keeps a few tormented souls awake through
    the night . . .

I am awake there with her, and the world sleeps around
    our bodies.

AGE

The years roll by and age advances.
The nights come one after another, and age advances.
Rains come after the summer, age advances—
The flowers of the spring bloom and age advances.

Sickness goes and sickness ceases to be.
In some mid-afternoon, sickness comes quietly to live in
   the bones.
In the quiet nights, somebody, it seems,
Knocks on the door of the heart noisily.
The plunderer forces itself in and releases
The storm of the universe breathing inside you, away
   from you . . .

31

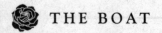

THE BOAT

How long you will go, how long you can go alone?
You will have to tie your boat to something on shore,
    somewhere.
Not only you, but the men who are born in water.

The man unbroken from a group is also alone. In solitude,
Resting the weary brain in the arms of the dark and
    deep night,
He still sits in an unfamiliar boat—

Sit empty-handed after giving away the remaining dimes
Love sells dear in this part of the world.

MANY YEARS, AND DEATH

For many years I stood face to face—
In front of my mother, my father, beloved people—
I have stood speechless for many years.
For many years I didn't know if I was alive,
For many years, the distance between living and not living
Moves to zero, pulled together like two thin threads
That live inside me. One is a terribly dumb, a Semal tree
Whose last dry leaf has fallen off, one
The spring that bid farewell from life like birth.
If I die tonight, nobody say anything,
Just put an epitaph under any Semal tree anywhere,
      a verse
Written by me long ago, white letters
On white paper.

YOU, ARANYA

1.

So strange . . . how can you disappear, just like that?
You know how desperately I desire you,
Even after wallowing for so long in the arbour of my lust,
You leave so easily, after night falls, throwing a simple 'See
    you' at me—
'Let's meet up again tomorrow' as you melt into the darkness.

What is the need to meet tomorrow?
Will tomorrow be any different?
Drinking to the hilt and getting me drunk,
Swinging roots before each cubicle
Of my body that craves your touch,
You speak of another day we will meet again
And I will keep listening.
You will go on speaking of the days to follow.

2.

Every day the next day will arrive and disappear,
We will keep talking about everything that has happened
    or is happening

Since the day of genesis to this nemesis day.
Revolutions will be brought about in the world
Of the destitute with thunderous thumping on my body—
A communion racing in any direction, from mud to
    mortuary, playground
To Mohana, whichever way you desire, and that too
    so agreeably.
Every day I will drink from those eyes of yours, little by little,
Rousing me to walk into the desert, alone.

3.

You smell like a lover, but you are not, Aranya
I want you to be one,
I want you to be with me the entire day,
The entire night.
There is no trace of such desire in your universe,
You are more niggardly than a red ant—
Not content with the winter accumulations,
You preserve yourself underneath, throughout the
    summer, rain and autumn.
Even the irresistible spring finds you unmoving.
Everything in me fascinates you
Except the me inside and this, my famished heart, that craves
The elephant musting beneath your lust.
Trampling me under feet, to the finish . . .

Set me free.
If you can't do that, give me love then and liberate me.
Come alive for once, O Aranya.

4.

I give you—without inhibition—my prose and my lines
    of verse.
You will trash it all one day, laugh it off
In the company of men.
You will tell them about the last time
I gave myself to you, when I knew
That any day hereafter, you could walk away—
Murderous in a moment.

5.

Not an iota of trust I waste on you,
Still every single cell of my skin yearns for your kisses,
My breasts ache to be roused into a passionate frenzy—
I need your explorations.
My inside and my outside wait for you,
My love waits for you, the flames

I know I fly into.
Still I fly, some souls so hapless.

Even after burning ourselves into ashes
We thirst for flames.
We'll beg to be burnt again.

6.

But you are no Greek god, Aranya!
I could have done without staring at you.
You are no horizon star.
I indulged in you a whole year, drank your liquor and light—
There is nothing like love in India, I know . . .

Let us name it lust for now and carry on with the kissing.
You are the squint-eyed, chauvinistic charlatan in
    your mid-forties,
Eager to finish the kissing with your eyes closed.
The magic of kissing can cure hypocrisy.
If I go and fall in love, it must be in me to fall in love.
Strolling side by side in the silver forest of moonlit
    midnight hours . . .
Can a hand resist the touch of another next to it?

7.

Let the frenzied excitement of wild histrionics go on,
Let tongues wag,

You know and I know,
To get together in bed shows just how much we have
    gone through.
You keep the woman of the house your sacred cow and
    flirt around outside.
It's in your blood, more than blood it's in
Each and every brain cell.
'See if you have time to sit and share a few words this
    spring,' I say, or
'Will you stop your hurricane drive after free liquor
    to stay awhile?'
Why must women speak with such expectations?
The chivalrous men in this Bengali burst out with pride
    before me
In the eulogy of those fawning wenches. But

Isn't my life my own?
I want to live it on my own terms, wild or whatsoever.
Even aware of all that you are, Aranya, I have
Always been alone, happy in my aloneness.
You stormed in turbulent and made me lonelier.
But let go of those accounts, other things, my matters.
You are not alone after all, your carnival runs through
    all seasons.
My heart is the worst enemy in the game.

8.

Lost in the ecstasy of your love, I didn't know of the
    disease you passed on to me.
I sealed my lips with yours for a kiss, didn't notice the
    poison you passed on to me covertly.

9.

With your disease inside me now I lie in the boat,
And you watch that boat inch towards death.
The drops of water pushing me under don't dampen your
    celebrations!
Those who love, those who don't understand the language
    of give and take, they
Float away to another shore
Where it rains fire.
You love to enjoy the sunset while drinking champagne,
    slowly
From a tall, thin glass.

# SURREY DREAMS

One by one, they've all gone.
Riding in the front seat of the carriage of time,
    everyone goes—
I stare at the backs of their heads—they empty
Their lives and go.

I am the only one who cannot go into a new life,
I stay behind, holding on to the past.
Everyone rolls with glee in this glittering world, they live
A fairy-tale life. I am the sole
One in the audience seat, everyone has gone
From my life, one by one: dried leaves in the balcony, dust
Drifting into one room, and another, cobwebs
    on photographs . . .
My companions for the life that is left.

I could not escape from any other life in this life.
The ones who have gone have forgotten, but I haven't.
I chant their memories and spend the rest of life
Like particles of light moving both towards life, and away.

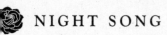

NIGHT SONG

I stay awake to stare at the night.
I stay up at night and listen to the stories of the night.

Some are afraid of the night and they move away.
Some get pulled by the threads of the night and inch closer.

Every night, the night gives company to the ones that stay
    awake, it stays awake.
It stays awake and gives dreams to the ones that sleep.

I stay awake at night and listen to the hustle of the night.
I stay up at night, listening for the wail of the day that lies
    on the other side of night.

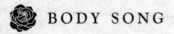

BODY SONG

The seasons visit.
Even now I can
Feel the eagerness
Of each body.

I don't know how much
Or how the hormones sense
Each movement of the bodies.

Awake the whole night, singing—
The soul is so dangerously
Dependent on the body.

VIBRATION SONG

I am still here.
Still seasonal.
Hungrily, I crave

The inch towards the thirties.
In my temperament, my behaviour,
I am extraordinarily
Bloody, I am the romance
Of the bees.

DELIRIUM SONG

One day, I shall build
A nest on the seashore
Or maybe in the mountains.

When the empty mist
Rolls down my exiled skies,
I shall drench myself in the deluge
Of a delirious fever.

Don't come to see me.
Don't come to see sickness . . .
One day, I shall devour myself.

DISTANCE SONG

Two people sleep
Next to each other, each

Stranger to the other within.
Who has birds fluttering and

Who locks cages within?
Who sleeps, and doesn't wake the night?

SELF-SONG

It is nature I worship—
The further I walk in the world of people, deception
Finds my sleeves and pulls me back
To the word that rests inside: alone.
If I could walk around the city in the dead
Of night and shed tears, alone, I'd still

Have no belief in God.
Religion-mongers make divides in the sly
Of homes. They keep aside women from humans.
I am paired with nothing but nature, which amazes me.
As for being born human, how well I also know
Men of probity, astute politicians who gather
Applause as they elocute on class exploitation
While carefully tucking away words on female abuse.

Religion has spread its tentacles, and an octopus
Is more beautiful. All my valiant solitude hardly moves a fig.

CHARACTER

You're a girl
And you better remember:
When you cross the threshold of your house,
Men will be suspicious.
When you keep on walking down the lane,
Men will whistle and follow the sway of your gait.
When you step on to the main road, crossing the lanes,
Men will revile you and call you a whore.

What is whore? Who makes the woman loose?

If you've got no character,
You'll turn back to the threshold
Of safety. Of iniquity. And if you have
Identity—your stamp, you'll keep on going
As you're going now.

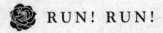 RUN! RUN!

A pack of dogs is after you.
Remember rabies.
Remember teeth and claws.
Remember their pack of howls.

A pack of men are after you.
Remember syphilis.
Remember teeth and claws.
Remember their pack of howls.

DIVIDED

Your father, your brother, your sister—
These are nothing to you. You are alone.
Aashi, Abhijit, Vyaka, Vrisa . . . your friends:
They, too, are nothing to you. You are
Alone. The moon above and the moon
Below. When you weep, your little finger
Wipes the tears from your eyes, and that finger is your own.
When you walk: your feet.
When you speak: your tongue.
When you laugh, your cheerful eyes are your only friends.

That milk tooth? It has abandoned you—
Except for yourself, you have no one,
No mammal or plant, no fish or bird.
There is a space in the rock waiting
For your fossil.

But as much as you
Say you are yours,
Are you really?

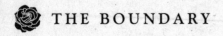

THE BOUNDARY

The square Earth became round at last—
After she was enlightened, and wished to see
The shape and sense and colour or the world,
She wanted to leap out over the threshold:
They told her—no. This wall is the horizon.
This roof terrace is your terrible sky.
This bed and bolster, scented soap, talcum powder,
This onion and garlic, this needle and thread—
Slow, lazy afternoons, embroidering, red and blue flowers
On the pillowcases—this partition is your only life.

When she opened the main gate's black padlock
To see the land in which she could've wandered
On that far-off shore,
They told her—no. Plant seedlings of sajne
    in the courtyard.
This will make men strong and healthy and total.
Spinach vine, bottle gourd, grow them here and there in
    various pots.
This courtyard of cactus and yellow roses with a stone-
    smooth floor,
This perfect portion is your one divided life.

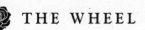

THE WHEEL

They dressed her in red, a flashy colour
Catching the eye. They tied a necklace at her throat.
    The necklace
Around the neck of a helpless animal is made of rope.
For feasts and festivals?
A necklace made of coarse and proper paper.

Her ears and nose have proper piercings, metal things
And the lustre of cheap gems. She's got so little lustre of
    her own.
These tiny shards of bric-a-brac brighten her up.

They put bangles on her wrists, their shapes so much
Like handcuffs, like shackles. The shining
Bracelets jingle on her ankles. When she moves,
Her whereabouts are known to all.
They apply paints to her face, light
And colour upon some lifeless thing
As if her eyes, her cheeks, her lips were not exact.
As if without this added colour she isn't enough, cannot
Be complete. A person is turned
Into merchandise like this, she's merchandise

In the villages, merchandise in town, she's product of the
        sidewalks, the streets,
She's produce in the slums, the aristocratic locales.
She's commerce in this country, and every place abroad.
In terrible ways at various rates, she's livestock.

She is sold, and
Sold openly! In some territories, the sales have been
        made modern.
Some applaud this modernization: women's progress.
        Women's expansion.

Most stupid women willingly tangle themselves in chains
To fulfil some desire. Those who break
The chains think that they have emerged—
These stupid women tangled in another darker chain.

ACQUAINTANCE

How much can you come
To know the real man?
As much as I had thought
Him to be a true male,
That much he is not:
Half neutered, he is half
A male. As life goes

By, and I sit and live and eat with a man—
He whom I so long thought I knew
Correctly—he whom I know is nothing
Like that; in fact, he's the one I most don't know.
How much can anyone know someone else?
How can a woman know what man is, truly?

Hair, eyes, mouth . . . but monster.
As much as I had thought him to be a man,
That much he is not; half beast
He is, half a man. Is there nothing
Whole in this life, on this Earth?

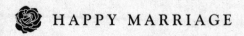

HAPPY MARRIAGE

My life,
Like a sandbar, has been rolled over
By a monster of a man. He wants
My body beneath him so that if he wishes he can slap
Me on the cheek,
Can spit in my face,
And roughly pinch my rear.
Like a rogue wave, he can rip off my clothes
And take the naked beauty in his grip.
If he wishes, he can pull out my eyes.
If he wishes, he can chain my feet,
If he wishes, he can, with no qualms whatsoever,
Whip on me like the wind.
If he wishes, he can chop off my hands, slice open
    my fingers.
If he wishes, he can salt my open wounds,
He can throw ground black pepper in my eyes. I am
    the wife
So, if he wishes, he can slash my thigh with a dagger,
String me up and hang me.

In my lonely house at night,
Sleepless, full of anxiety, clutching

54

At the window grill,
He wanted my heart under his control,
I would wait for him and sob.
He poured himself over my heart
So that I would love him.
My tears rolling down, I bake home-made bread;
He wanted my heart so that I would drink, as if
They were ambrosia, the filthy liquids
Of his philandering body, so that, loving him, I would melt
   like wax.
Not turning my eyes towards any other man,
I would give proof of my chastity all my life.
So that, loving him, on some moonlit
Night, I would die by suicide
In a fit of ecstasy.

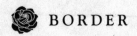

BORDER

My child is pulling at my sari,
My husband stands blocking the door—
But I will go. I'm going to move ahead.
Behind me my whole family is calling.

There's nothing ahead but a river
I will cross.
I know how to swim, but they
Won't let me swim, won't let me cross . . .

And there's nothing on the other side of the river
But a vast expanse of fields.
But I'll embrace this empty space
And run against the wind, whose howl
Makes me want to dance. I'll dance someday.
And then return

To play keep-away (something not done for years)
As I did in childhood.
I'll raise a wonderful commotion playing keep-away
    someday
When I return.

For years I haven't cried with my head
In the lap of solitude, I'll cry
To my heart's content someday
And then return to the river that breaks
This line between nothing and myself.
There's nothing ahead but this river—
And I know how to swim.
Why shouldn't I go? I'll go.

WITH A BAD DREAM YESTERDAY

Late yesterday evening in the Bangla Academy field
I met a bad dream eating peanuts, joking with his pals.
Shuffling a few peanut shells in his left hand
As if about to throw them like dice. I gazed into the
     bad dream's
Eyes—eyes the hazy colour of darkness just beginning.

Marijuana smoke twisted into rings in the wind, entwining
With my scarf, and in my dreamy eyes, then, the smoky
     sky itself.
And on the forehead of that sky
One lakh dots of sandal paste.
Suddenly, not giving a damn about anyone, the bad dream
Grabbed me, pulled me into his arms and devoured
Me with thirty-nine kisses, counting out loud all the
     while, his bronze hair
Blowing in a fantastic wind,
The buttons of his shirt open, his chest
Drenched in the light of the moon.
I stumbled home after midnight, and the bad dream
     tagged
Along with me, murmuring all the way about love.

The bad dream is totally shameless, and at once
The deliverer of shame and delirium . . .

The night passed, and then the day. I awoke
But the bad dream remains—never once saying 'I love
      you', and
I knew then like I know now he would never leave.

THE FAULT OF LONELINESS

My fingernails grow longer, my ankles are weak—
My hair is a mess with neglect, my arms thin and pale.
Renouncing everything, I am vanishing inside and out.
Far away from the world in this isolated place,
     I am exile itself.
In my single room, even the wind is afraid to knock.
A few dogs used to howl in the middle of the night,
Or briefly at noon. But one day even they got up
And left my darkening compound.

I know all about your lechery.
You are a cheat, a hypocrite from head to toe.
But even so, it's the fault of loneliness that I go to you.
Immersing in your dirty water, I smear my body with
     flawless disgrace.
Everyone knows about your mistaken love.
Even so, it's the fault of loneliness I go,
Knocking again at your door.

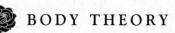

BODY THEORY

In the house of my nerves, a bell chimes.
This body of mine, known so long . . .
At times, even I can't recognize it.
If rough hands with various tricks touch my sandal paste-
    smeared hand,
A bell chimes.

This body tells its story in its own language, words
I can't read; these fingers, eyes, these lips, these smooth feet,
None of those are mine.
This hand is mine, yet I don't correctly recognize this hand.
These lips are mine. These are my breasts, buttocks, thighs;
None of these muscles, none of these pores,
Are under my command or my control.
In the two-story house of my nerves.
A bell chimes.

In this world, whose plaything am I, then,
Man's or nature's? Which theory do I know, do I study?

In fact, not man but nature
Plays me, I am the sitar of its whims.

At man's touch, I wake
Up, breaking out of my slumbering childhood;
In my wild sea, a sudden high tide begins.
If the sweet scent of love is found in my blood and flesh,
It's nature only that plays me,
I am the sitar of its whims.

AT THE BACK OF PROGRESS

The fellow who sits in the air-conditioned office
Is the one who in his youth
Raped a dozen or so young girls.
This is the evening of great success, great catastrophe.
At the cocktail party he is stricken with lust, and fastens
His eyes on the belly button of some lovely thing.
In the five-star hotel, this fellow tries
Out his different moves, engages his salacious tastes—
Tries to make it with a variety of women.
This fellow then goes home and beats
His wife over a misfolded handkerchief
Or a soggy shirt collar.
In the dark, early morning, this fellow sits
In his office and chats with the people who work for him
While puffing on a cigarette
And shuffling through his files.
Ringing the small bell on his enormous desk, he calls
His secretary, shouts at him, orders the tea to be hotter
And drinks. Later, he vouches for a friend who's just
      been fired.

No one knows or would ever suspect
His vile behaviour, his wandering evil.

Gathering with his buddies, he buys some movie tickets.
The film ends. Kicking back on the porch outside,
   he indulges
In loud harangues on politics, art and literature.
   His friends look
At one another and say nothing. Some things need no
   explanation.

But in another world, also his, someone
Is committing suicide. His mother, or his grandmother
Or his great grandmother.

Returning home, he beats his wife
Over a bar of cracked soap or
The baby's nagging cough.

The bearer who brings the tea
And keeps the lighter in his pocket
Gets a couple of taka as a tip . . . and still
Our fellow has divorced his first wife for her sterility,
His second wife for giving birth to a daughter—
He's left his third wife for not bringing a dowry. Another
   film ends. Returning
Home, this fine fellow beats his fourth wife
Over a few overripe chillies or a handful of
   too-cooked rice.

At the other end of progress something bursts
From the seams of the Earth, devours anything in its sight
And presses on into the body of a woman torn in two.

AGGRESSION

Human nature has no lesson.
If you sit, they'll say—'No, don't sit.'
If you stand, 'What's the matter, walk!'
And if you walk, 'Shame on you, sit down!'
Circle of life in a life in circles.

If you so much as lie down, no respite—'Get up.'
If you don't lie down, they'll bother you: 'Lie down for a bit'
And peel you back, one layer at a time.

I'm wasting my days getting up and sitting down.
The circle makes a square against my grave.
If I'm dying right now, they speak up—'Live.'
If they see me living, who knows when
They'll say—'Shame on you, die!'

In tremendous fear, I secretly go on living.

SOMETHING OR OTHER

Some gluttonous men
Who think that women are fresh cuts of veal,
Who think we are mango jelly, boiled eggs or
Sweets made of milk, are something or other,

One thing or another. Some sick men
Think of women as diseases, stagnant pools,
Garbage dumps of parasites.
They think of us as inferior
Forlorn creatures of the earth, one
And another amongst themselves, desperate for a cure.

Some religious fanatic cowards
Think of women as grotesque life forms
Fashioned from men's leftover ribs,
Tasty morsels offered up for amorous sport, one
Or many gathered in the kitchen, starving.

There'll always be some shit in this world,
Some fetid essence or another, something
In the hollow wind against which we walk.

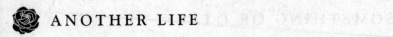

ANOTHER LIFE

Picking lice from each other's hair
The women spend the afternoon
Squatting on the porch.
A committee of vultures, a gaggle of geese . . .
What is the name for a group of women?
They spend the evening feeding
Children and loving them to sleep in the glow of
     the bottle
Lamp. The rest of the night they give their backs
To be slapped and kicked by the man of the house
Or sprawl, half-naked, on a hard wooden cot—

Crows and women greet the dawn together.
Women blow into the oven to start the fire,
Tap on the back of the winnowing tray with five fingers
And with two fingers pick out stones.
Crows sit in gangs on the line, black on black.
A flock of ravens? An unkindness.
Owls? A parliament. A host of sparrows.

Women spend half of their lives picking stones from rice.

Stones pile up in their hearts,
There's no one to touch them with two fingers . . .
No wing on which to fly towards their murder.

FIRE AND HUSBAND

The dictionary says that he's my
Chief, lord, master, etc. etc.
Society agrees: he's my only God.

My senile husband has learned well
The prevailing rules and regulations, he exerts authority.
He's eager to stroll over the bridge of eternity
To the glittering realm of his paradise: All kinds of fruits,
Brightly coloured cordials and delicious foods
He lusts after the fair-skinned bodies of houris to chew,
    suck and lick.

Nothing's written on my forehead but your dark faith.
I spend my lifespan in society, thrusting
Chunks of firewood into the oven of these earthly days.
In the afterlife, I see my doddering husband
Exult over the seven-seven pleasures of sex.

I am alone, in the joyous gardens of paradise I am alone.
Watching the blind obscenity of men,
I burn inside in the everlasting fires of hell—
A chaste and virtuous woman.

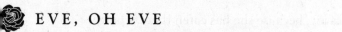

EVE, OH EVE

A tongue to feel thirst,
A heart with which to love . . .
Why would Eve suppress her wishes?
Why won't Eve eat of the fruit?

Didn't Eve have a stomach with which to feel hunger?
Didn't she have a hand to reach out with,
Fingers with which to make a fist?

Then why won't Eve eat of the fruit?

Because Eve has eaten of the fruit
She must regulate her steps,
Subdue her thirst.
She is compelled.
To keep Adam walking through the garden of Eden
All their lives.

There are sky and earth,
Because she has eaten.
There are moon, sun, rivers and seas.
Because Eve has eaten: trees, plants and vines,
Because she has eaten of the fruit

There is joy, because she has eaten there is pure
Joy, unadulterated laughter, the innocent child dancing.
Eating the fruit from the glorious tree, Eve made a heaven
    of earth.

Eve, if you get hold of the fruit,
Don't ever refrain from eating.

THINGS CHEAPLY HAD

In the market, nothing can be had
As cheaply as women.
With a small bottle of *alta* for their feet—
Surely, these days, made from nothing natural,
Synthetic oils and artificial dye—
They spend three nights sleepless with Joy.
For a few bars of soap to scrub their skin
And some scented oil for their hair
Women become so submissive that they scoop
Out chunks of their flesh
To be sold in the flea market twice a week.
If they get a jewel for their nose
They lick a man's feet for seventy days or so—
A full three-and-a-half months
If it's a single striped sari.

Even the mangy cur of the house barks
Now and then, but over the mouths of women
There's a lock, a golden lock, pasted gold
With the weight of heaven and hell.

SHAME, 7 DECEMBER 1992

A gang of men with *tupi*s on their heads, stormed
Into Satipada's house, poured
Gasoline over everything, the tables and chairs,
The beds, wardrobes, pots and pans,
Clothing, books. The gang then quickly lit
A box of matchsticks. And tossed them.

The plan was that Satipada Das would come
To my house that morning for tea and snacks.
We would play chess and gossip
To our hearts' content. Satipada comes
Every day, but not today . . . the news came through
    instead of him.

As the fires flared up
In all the gasoline-soaked places, Satipada
Stood in the courtyard and watched
The black smoke spreading over the Tati Bazar, over
Satipada's patch of indifferent sky.

In the evening, I went to Satipada's house and saw
Him sitting alone upon the ash and charred wood

Of his forefather's ancestral home, blood running down.
His body, dark bruises on his chest and back.

Out of shame I could not touch him.

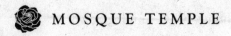

MOSQUE TEMPLE

Let the pavilions of religion be ground to bits—
Let the bricks of temples, mosques, gurudwaras,
    churches—
Be burned in blind fire,
And upon those heaps of destruction make
Lovely flower gardens grow, spreading their fragrance,
Let children's schools and study halls grow there.

For the welfare of humanity, now let prayer halls
Be turned into hospitals, orphanages, schools, universities,
Now let prayer halls become academies of art, fine arts
    centres,
Scientific research institutes,
Now let prayer halls be turned to golden rice fields
In the radiant dawn, open fields, rivers, restless seas.

From now on, let religion's other name be humanity.

NOORJAHAN

They have made Noorjahan stand in a hole
    in the courtyard—
There she stands, submerged to her waist,
    her head hanging.
They are throwing stones at Noorjahan.
Those stones are striking my body—

Pounding my head, forehead, chest and back.
They are throwing stones and laughing aloud, laughing
    and shouting abuse.
Noorjahan's eyes have burst. My eyes
Have burst. Noorjahan's nose has been smashed,
    and my nose
Has been broken, is bleeding.
Through Noorjahan's torn breast,
    her heart has been pierced . . .
Are these stones not striking you?

They are laughing and stroking their beards. One man
Smokes a pipe while another sips his tea, and smiles.
There are *tupis* on their heads and they, too, are shaking
    with laughter.
They're laughing and swinging their walking sticks;

From the quiver of their eyes, cruel arrows speed to pierce
    her body,
My body, the young girl's body, the body of the women
    one thousand miles from here . . .
Are these arrows not piercing your body?

CANNONADE

There are forts made of stone, made of brick, made
By the backs of men who, after those terrible days of labour
Went home to women cooking and ate from them
    in silence.

Special branch guards are on twenty-four-hour duty in
    front of my door.
They write down everything in a small, green notebook.
Who comes and who goes, when I leave, when I enter—
Who my friends are, whose waist I embrace as I laugh—
Whom I whisper to . . . everything.
But there are things they cannot record:
Which thoughts come and go in my head,
What it is that I nurture in my consciousness.

The government has cannons and rifles.
And a little mosquito like me has a sting.

IF YOU'RE IN LOVE, PLEASE GO ON . . .

'Without a sky, a place where human faces are faceless—
Like a world of dead eyes in starless darkness
Where I will pierce myself with poison arrows
And destroy this one life—
A raging train of loneliness will end all that was and
        could be.'
That's what you said would happen
If I left . . . that you would die.

But you were the one who walked away,
Leaving behind the lies that made you blind,
And I never once called you back. I thought
You would turn back, so I waited the whole day—afternoon
And night. Don't think I had nowhere to go.
I did not move because I did not want to.
Where you left me? That's where I stood, colder
Quieter, till I was cold and blank as stone.

Perhaps you were trying to drag
Living out of your life, there in a dark cave
Somewhere dank, or on the railway tracks.
A serpentine anxiety curled around my stony body and clung.

The morning dew was still trembling on the green blade,
The fields were still deep in slumber.
To my surprise I found you, kneeling by a houri's feet
Like Krishna enticing the maiden
With the same old lines and rhymes.

A YEAR SPENT IN LOVE

Days and nights spent in love, in physical pleasures—
Every moment immersed in the thoughts of a distant man—
A year passed, unwittingly.

And then one day, it dawned on me in a morning flash:
I was nothing but a companion
For his insomnia, his strange blindness,
    his lust and loneliness.
Anyone can be that companion, he can sit
Beside anyone, he can love anyone and cling like a bat
To their lives worth something more than mine.

Who will bring me back those days?
The bat clung to my heart, nibbled on my heart
And breast with its poison teeth . . .
And I did not even see it for years!

He can set himself adrift with anyone he wants,
But I can only swim against the tide of myself.
He can ward off his loneliness even in the black cave colony,
Slinging from woman to woman.
All he needs is someone
To immerse himself in, a place for his fang.

Which nights has he not spent upside-down somewhere?
Which nights has he spent gazing at the rain,
With eyes wet with tears?

When you roll over, breathless, to rest a bit,
    or get up to bathe,
You will find he has flown again
To some other body, a small hole
Still over your heart where the blood has turned black.

They have weapons, so they start a war.
They love to destroy, so they have started the war.

Let's kiss, and show
The warmongers our middle fingers.
Wet with kisses, we each of us blossom into a country.
Your name is Russia. Me? Ukraine.
It's not so insane . . . if you are Cuba, El Salvador, Nicaragua,
If you are Panama,
If you are Iraq, Afghanistan,
I am America.
You are Israel today. I am Palestine.
Carnation, calla Lily, yellow columbine.
I am India, you China.
Let's kiss, let's tell barbarity and brutality
    to go fuck themselves.

If you collect all the weapons of the world—
All the nukes of the world—
And put them against our national kisses,
You will surely be a loser.
One simple kiss—one petal—is more powerful
Than the fucked-off blood of anger, of missiles.

Let's kiss, let's
Make love, let's work hard to make it right—
Our child will be born, and we will name
This child: 'Earth'.

THOSE LIPS, THAT TONGUE

You did not love me though you said you did.
For months and years those lips, that tongue—they bear
Witness. There's no true sign, no witness.

But my body and the favourite sari not touched in ages,
The comb, the kohl, the tears night after night.

Those who profess love without love . . .
I have always wanted to see what kind of people they are.
They walk like others, return home, sleep.
They, too, read newspapers over morning tea,
They listen to music, they have families.

Every time my heart has tried to touch
Your heart, it runs into those lips, that tongue,
And taking them as you, found joy in it.
For months, years, it has done so.
My poor, beating heart. My blind, savage heart!

Who will let my one heart know
That it was only your lips, your tongue?
Who will reveal that they have only learned
To utter words, a few meaningless letters?

I hide, both from you and myself
Perhaps from the very moment of birth.
Death can speak in tongues we never hear.

# LOVE UNFURLED

If I have to put kohl on my eyes for you,
And colour my hair and my face,
Douse myself in perfume,
And unfurl my best sari—
If I have to don garlands and bangles,
Tuck in my belly, hide the creases under my chin
Or in the corner of my eyes,
Then what I have for with you has come undone.

If ever it was something kept and blessed.
All the flaws, all the mistakes and ugliness, let them all be
What I am and what I will. I stand in front of you to
    be loved
Beyond the mirror made in something I am not.

WALKING THROUGH THIS LIFE AND INTO DEATH

1.

Death stands just beyond the window.
The moment I open the door,
It looks me blankly in the eyes.
If I sit, it finds a seat beside me, there
In the tea shop or relaxing in the bazaar.
Death is watching me and smiling.
I hear it in the water running in the restroom sink,
It quietly whispers its name and address
Late in the afternoon as I step out
In crowded markets, whichever way
I turn, under each sky I walk
It clings to me. Near palaces, in the slums—
I breathe it swiftly into my lungs.
What choice do I have otherwise?

2.

Let me live a few more days, a few more months,
Give me a few more years Death, my darling,

Only a few more years—
Once I finish the work at hand, I will not turn you away.

If you give me five more, that will be best.
Will you? What harm have I done you?
So much I will be able to get done in five years!
Now, if I get around seven or eight . . .
A decade would be best. Will you give me ten more,
    darling?
If you are fine with ten, what difference
Would two more years make?
So, give me twelve—those too shall pass in a blink.

So, Death, you magician, could you not give me
Fifteen or twenty, simply out of love?
Those too shall pass.
A year hardly takes a year to go by.

You have surrounded me on all sides,
Who knows what brings about what?
If I had freedom, would I have begged
For more or less? I could have done as I pleased,
But now no one seems to want to let me live.
You stand over me with a dark cane,
Nothing is as it used to be. I know
You want to live too, Death, in this one world.

And me? If you have mercy, I will live out each day
In debt to your clemency.
So, give me a few years, my darling,
Let me write to my heart's content—
Just a few more lines against death before I die.

3.

They have come out with spears and machetes,
Swords and venomous snakes, religion
On their minds, hate in their hearts
Pistols tucked in their waists.
They will kill me to save their religion.

For no less than a thousand years
Man has killed to save religion.
Bathed in human blood
People have spread religious creed from one
Nation to the next and then the next.
It was humans who did it,
It was humans who made religion
Bigger than humanity itself, wrote the godly texts
And made these inert books cannibals.
If the spirit were truly free, it would have screamed
And called for you, Death. If religion had life,
It would have died from shame

Two thousand years ago
For humankind, for our greater good.

4.

There's no one on the other side.
Perhaps there is no other side at all.
Death will not take me anywhere, to no court,
It will not stand me in front of a door
Beyond which there rest the humours of the body
Or some fountain of endless delights.

When I bid farewell to the universe,
My body will lie in the morgue.
And once the autopsy is done,
My bones and remains will be sold in bulk
Just to crumble one day and become dust,
Dust that will disappear into the dusk.

Those who believe in that other side,
Let them go, place a kiss on Death
And knock on the bric-a-brac door,
Where unending glory awaits them.
Let me stay on this transient earth,
Its forests, mountains and wild seas,
Let me sleep on the grass and the wildflowers,

Let me wake with the songs of birds
And wrap myself in golden sunlight—
Let me laugh and love under the full moonlight.
Let me walk among the crowds, in the rain, and let me live.

Those who are happy with the other side, let them be.
Even if I must endure sorrow on this earth,
This world is my here and my hereafter.

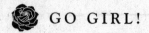
GO GIRL!

They said—'Take it easy,'
Said—'Calm down,'
Said—'Stop talking, shut up!'
They said—'Sit down, bow your head,'
Said—'Keep on crying, let the tears roll . . .

What should you do in response?

You should stand up now—
Should stand right up, hold
Your back straight, hold
Your head high . . .
You should speak,
Speak your mind,
Speak it loudly . . .
Scream!

You should scream so loud that they must run for cover.
They will say—'You are shameless!'
When you hear that, just laugh . . .

They will say—'You have no moral character!'
When you hear that, just laugh louder . . .

94

They will say—'You are rotten!'
So just laugh, laugh even louder . . .

Hearing you laugh, they will shout,
'You are a whore!'

When they say that,
just put your hands on your hips, stand
Firm and say, 'Yes, yes, I am a whore!'

They will stare in disbelief.
They will wait for you to say more, so much more . . .

The men amongst them will turn red and sweat.
The women amongst them will dream to be a whore
    like you.

I took a chance and told you how much
I wanted to sail free upon the waters of life.
You said, 'What the hell will we get out of it?
We will only get wet, catch a cold.'

Don't worry, my dearest, we'll soon
Venture out to the open sea. But for now,
Let us stay here where I can wrap
Myself in your body's tender warmth . . .

For a full year, I let you warm yourself
With my fragrance until you sank
My dream of sailing upon
Waters of love, drowned me in silence.

There was a boat; there were oars.
The sail, too, had caught wind.
But I spent all my time on land
Wearily towing the barge of your life.

THE ROOM IN WHICH I AM
FORCED*

The room in which I now live has a closed window, one
That I cannot open at will. And this window is covered
With heavy curtains that cannot be moved.

I live in this room now. It is a room
Whose door cannot be opened at will,
A threshold that cannot be crossed.
Yes, I live in this room.

Two sickly lizards crawl all over the walls.
No man—nor any creature resembling a man—
Is permitted to enter here.

I now live in the foul air of this room struggling
Just to breathe. There's no sound at all
     except for the banging
Of my head against the wall.

No one else in the world sees me

---

* Written while Taslima was forced to live in confinement in Delhi from
22 November 2007 to 19 March 2008.

But that odd couple of old lizards.
They watch me with wide eyes open
To the room and the rest of the world.
Who knows if they can feel my pain?
When I cry, their old, seeing eyes seem filled with tears.

I live in this room where what is called democracy
Forces me to live for days unending.
It is a room in the uncertain dark—
The threat of death hanging by its green, thin tail.
In pain, breathing with difficulty, where democracy
Forces me to live, the secular world outside
Drains me of life, drop by drop.
It is a lizard cage where my dear India
Has forced me to stay. I do not know

If these busy men—these creatures that almost look
     like men—
Possess a few seconds to spare
For the lifeless lump that will one day
Arise from this reptile room.
I'm a rotten, greasy lump of bones . . .

Will death be my release?
Perhaps death will set me free—
Free at last to cross the threshold of this suffocation.

The lizards stare. Maybe they will feel sad

When someone buries me:
Maybe it will be a government man
Who will wrap me in the flag of democracy
And put me down in the soil of my dear India.
At long last I'll find a home there,
With no threshold to cross . . .
No old lizards to bear witness . . .
Yes, I'll find a home there
Where breathing will come without pain.

TERROR*

Soldiers, rifles in hand, encircle me.
I stand in their midst, unarmed.

The soldiers don't know me; from time to time
They stare so strangely
At what they see is a woman with no weapons . . .

None of them have a clue as to why I'm so suddenly here.
Dirty body, grimy clothes, depressed and unkempt hair.
I wear no chains the eye can see, but somewhere holding
    me back
Are the shackles this world has locked around my neck.

The soldiers sense my fear; they feel their rifles,
The weight of them the government knows
Are meant to strike terror in my heart.
Their bayonets, their boots—
The soldiers are only doing their duty,
But the men behind the iron desks
Would be so dreadfully upset

---

* Written while Taslima was forced to live in confinement in Delhi from
  22 November 2007 to 19 March 2008.

If they couldn't find a million ways
To strike terror in my heart.

I do not have the right to terrorize
The politicians, but they have the right to terrorize me.

I suppose the soldiers could inform their superiors
That this helpless unarmed woman refuses to be terrorized—
Tries to snap her invisible chains. If so, these

Politicians would order me to be hanged.
And once the day and time for the hanging is fixed,
They'd try to feed me fish curry, hilsa and shrimp.

But what if, at that very moment, I declare that I won't eat?
What if I don't moan in fear upon the gallows?
What if I have enough guts not to be terrorized—
Even when those same officials ring the noose around
     my neck!

WE*

Last night, a lizard sprang up from nowhere and landed upon me. It squirmed along my arm and then climbed upon my shoulder before inching towards my head and hiding itself in the dishevelled bush of my hair. Resting upon the back of my aching head, it kept gawking for a couple of hours at a second lizard. Then, at the stroke of dawn, it slid next to my ear, before deciding to squat upon my spine.

The second lizard lay frozen upon my right leg, around two inches below my knee. Neither budged from their positions the entire evening. Having failed to remove them, I did what I normally do. I kept lying with my eyes firmly closed. Silently—and even if there's really no rationale whatsoever for counting in reverse—I counted from hundred to one, repeatedly.

My bed is a confused mess of dirty clothes, used trays and cracked bowls with leftover meals . . . notebooks for scribbling, old newspapers that have turned brown because of tea stains; one or two combs with stray hairs sticking to

---

* Written while Taslima was forced to live in confinement in Delhi from 22 November 2007 to 19 March 2008.

them; one or two puffed rice crackers that have lost their crispness; scattered strips of pills and phials of potions; inkless pens etc., etc., etc.

For a number of days, more than two hundred black ants have occupied my bed. They have girded up their loins to construct their new colony upon my bed. Millimetre by millimetre, they have begun to take full control over me, as if digging tunnels in an ant farm. Shrivelled in fear, for days on end, I myself have become as tiny as these ants. I'm utterly stunned at their demeanour. They've been performing ballet programmes in classical styles upon the surface of my body—but not once have I been bitten, even by mistake.

I believe they've taken it for granted that I belong to them. And I've also begun to consider that perhaps, just perhaps, I am actually safer in their company than that of humans.

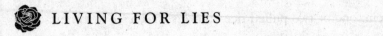

LIVING FOR LIES

If you tell the truth, people get angry—
Don't tell the truth any more, Taslima.
This time is not the time of Galileo.
This is the twenty-first century, but tell
The truth and nations force you to leave.
The State will put you in prison,
Torture you. Don't tell the truth . . .

Say the sun revolves around the earth.
Say the moon has its own light, like the sun.
Say the mountains are nailed to the earth so that the earth
does not fall into empty space.
Claim that women are made from ribs of men, insist
One neck bone of the women is crooked.
Claim all men and women will suddenly wake from
      their graves
And rise into youthful splendour, going to heaven
Or hell for eternity. Just lie, Taslima.

Say stars, planets and satellites, universe and gravity are
      thunderous lies.
Say man never landed on the moon which is, of course,
      made from cheese.

Simply lie. If you lie, you will no longer be in exile.
You will have a country of your own, have friends.
Will be free from the chains of reality, you will see
Light, and breathe the night air.
No one will throw you into exile—
So, never tell the truth, Taslima.

THE UNRUNG RING

So many things ring,
The cells of the body,

The ankle bells as they dance—
The silver bangles on the wrist.

As the monsoon rains fall on the window
The glass panes musically ring.

Clouds clash with clouds
And lightning rings out. Dreams

Ring, keeping time to their beats
And, creating havoc and beauty.

Loneliness rings. Only an intimate bell
On my door is silent—will never ring.

GIRL FROM SWITZERLAND

At the dinner party, everyone
Holds a glass of champagne or
White wine. All in a row, the big guys
Come up to shake my hand and hear how

I came out alive from the troglodyte's den.
Some want my autograph, some look at me
With wide-eyed admiration—
Some kiss, some offer flowers.

In the midst of all this,
A girl with golden hair extends her hand.
She doesn't want to hear my sad stories.
She has come, she says, to weep with me a while.
And I felt then the entire Brahmaputra
Rising in my throat on to the banks
Of my awe-filled eyes.

I, from the east, and she, from
The west, had pains that were equally deep.
I was dark, she a rosy white,
But our sorrows were equally blue.

Before we wept, we did not have to
Hear each other's miseries.
We knew about them all too well in silence.

GARMENT GIRLS

The garment girls, walking together,
Look like hundreds of birds flying
Through the Bangladeshi sky.

Garments girls, returning to their slums at midnight,
Are met by street-vagabonds who give a few
Takas to the girls, pushing their own bodies
Into the girl's bodies, stealing
The night's spoils. But this night is sleepless—

Before dawn, the girls again walk together,
Men's mouths watering to spit when they pass,
The girls avoiding as much as they can.
Eating no one's food, wearing no one's clothes, walking,
    walking on.

Like blind cattle, they trudge ahead,
Have-nots dependent upon the haves,
Forbidden to enjoy the sky's rainbows.
Fated to be thrown around, fingered, raped in darkness
    and fear
Instead of bathing joyfully in the moonlit night.

Like all of Bangladesh flying in the world's sky,
The garment girls walk on, walk on, and away and into
    air itself.

SHAME IN THE YEAR 2000

Eleven Muslim men
Are raping Purnima
In broad daylight, raping

Her, as Purnima is Hindu.
They are raping Purnima in the courtyard
Of her own home, they have tied

Purnima's mother to a bamboo post in her room—
Through a broken window slit she can see
Her teenage daughter's widened eyes and

Body writhing in pain. Purnima's sister lies
On her face holding tightly to her mother.
The flags of religion wave boldly

On eleven aroused phalluses. The mother's wails rise
Above Purnima's: 'Do whatever you want
with me but let Purnima be!'

The Muslims did not let Purnima be.
The moon will soon rise over the mosque
And Isha prayer will be held for all who come.

First, they cut open her stomach and took
The foetus out. With two hands, with two bloodied hands
The throat was slit, the head then pierced
On to the trident and they danced together, the patriotic

Citizens of a possible Hindu state danced together.
Someone threw the arms and legs of the still
Beating foetus—threw the pieces one by one
The torso, the trunk—all over her, the girl

Who screamed to live, who
Still wanted to live even when broken and hollow.
They were still dancing, dancing
And laughing while setting her on fire.
The girl burned, was burning to coal . . .

Her hair burned, flesh burned, bones burned to red coal,
Her heart, her lungs, her uterus burned to coal, and then
    to ash.

The trident has been staked above the ashes.
On the trident still lies pierced the unborn Muslim.
The Earth moves beneath us, but we don't feel it turn
Until some God we do not know whispers in our ears.

NOT A POEM

When my ma was dying, my father got ready, dressed up and left just like any other day. My elder brother had six flat breads fried in refined oil with a plateful of well-cooked mutton for breakfast. He could do with nothing less. My younger brother was warming his hands over the breasts and lips of a woman while pulling her towards himself. My elder sister-in-law had just applied a mask of turmeric paste all over herself, an effort to lighten her skin colour. Her instructions to servants for the day's lunch was issued: fried hilsa and a special recipe hotchpotch. My nephews were busy in the park outside smashing the cricket ball for boundaries and revelries. My other sister—an earnest homemaker—walked out with her children and husband for the children's park. My mother's brothers thrust their hands under my ma's pillow looking for the stray gold bangles and five-hundred-rupee notes.

The television kept blurting out Tibetan toothpaste and Pakeeza sari commercials in the empty room. Curious people popped in their heads on their way past. I was on the terrace mulling on strong words for a wonderful poem on feminism as I puffed on to a cigarette.

Ma died.

My father came back and changed. My elder brother finished his breakfast and let out a loud burp of pleasure. My younger brother got done with his woman and alighted from the bed. My elder sister-in-law had her bath, came out with her hair wrapped in a towel and enjoyed the fried hilsa and the hotchpotch that she had ordered. The nephews came back from the park. My other sister also returned from the children's park. My ma's brothers did nothing and waited. I came down from the terrace. The children sat in a row in front of the television for the daily soap. The elders had one eye on ma and the other on the television. The eye on ma was dry, the one on the television was wet from the last soap scene tragedy.

AMERICA

When you will be ashamed, America?
When will you wake up, America?
When will you stop your own terror, America?
When will you let the people of this world live, America?
When will you consider humans as humans, America?
When will you let the world simply be, America?
Powerful America, your bombs kill people yesterday
Today and tomorrow, decimate cities, grind civilization
To a halt. Your bombs kill possibilities and prostitutes alike,
Your bombs detrude dreams. When will you look

America at your own ceremony of massacre,
    your obscene mind?
At scandals crafted at your own behest?
When will you regret, America?
When will you be truthful, America?
When will you be human, America?
When will you cry, America?
America, when will you ask for forgiveness?

We are hurling hatred at you, America, we shall keep
Hurling that same hatred until you destroy all
Your weapons and fall on your knees.

Until you atone for your deeds, our children, our children's
Children will hate what you are—there is no deliverance

From this hatred, America. You have killed thousands of
    your own Indians,
You have killed in El Salvador, you have killed in
    Nicaragua,
Killed in Chile, in Cuba, in Panama, in Indonesia, in Korea.
You have killed in the Philippines, you are killing in Iran,
    Iraq, Libya, Greece, Palestine,
Sudan, Afghanistan—count the deaths, America, you
    need to keep count.
When will you hate yourself, America?
Hate yourself, there is still time.
Even now there is time to hide your face in your palms,
Even now there is time to hide yourself behind a bush
Or in the depths of a green forest, there is still time
To stay curled in shame, wrinkle up in a corner . . .
America, will you ever kill yourself?

But stop! Wait a moment, America!
You are democracy, you are freedom!
You're Jefferson's America, Lincoln's America,
Stand up, America, stand up for once, for the one last
Time, stand up for humanity, stand up for the world.

TO LIVE

In the abyss of eternal darkness, in a strange exile
I lie unmoving—there is no one to come for me.

I stare at the moon like the pied crested cuckoo.
The moon has learned to trick me, pouring
Silver darkness on my life as she runs from me—yet,
    I plead
Each night for her to come back. But why would the moon
Bother? Even humans can't find a few moments
To return, to be with their own people . . . why would
    the moon
Change her tune, why would she make room for my heart?

The winds from the south rush to silence me—
But I have lived in exile with the wind.
I do not yearn for anything from the skies. What can they be
But an endless nothingness?
I have enough of nothingness in India, in exile.

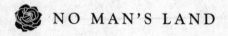

NO MAN'S LAND

If your own country does not
Give you spirit, which other country
In the world do you think will?
From country to country, the powers
Are the same. The ones who rule pierce you
With a thousand needles. They stone-face your sobs
While their innards dance in joy.
They are named differently, but the darkness
Gives them away—their lies, their laws, their footsteps
All tell you who they are.
When they run with the wind, the wind whispers who
    they are.
Rulers will be rulers, after all.

However much you've been told, a country
Does not belong to those who rule.
It belongs to the people who have built it in their hearts,
Who have drawn its maps with their toil and dreams!
Where do you go if the ones who rule drive you away?
Which country opens doors for the chased?
Which country will bring itself to you?

If you are no one any more, what
Do you have to lose? This is the time
To pull the world out and ask
For place, for the two feet to place themselves—a place to
    live.
The little pieces of no man's land that remain
After all boundaries are marked, that piece
Of unwanted land that none claims . . . let that be your
    country now.

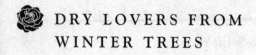

DRY LOVERS FROM
WINTER TREES

I have wanted to rake the dry leaves and set them on fire.
In the dead of night, I pick up the fire in my palms.
The dead stare of their ashes gives me goosebumps.
The dead leaves have lost the strings that kept them on
    the trees,
And float with the wind, sway over my balcony in
    playful mirth—
Headlong against the windows, all over my being, they are
    laughing aloud,
Whispering in my ear: *time to shed, time to shed.*
I put off setting them on fire, but I don't know why . . .

Perhaps it's because I can hear them quietly crying beneath
Those whispers, a wailing rupture of the ageless silence
    of lifeless
Deserts across the horizons to the ocean, where waves rise
    and fall.
Some walk, and walk into my lonely being
For a moment or two, but they have come nonetheless.
Maybe you have only stopped over on the way
To someplace else, but to me you came, nonetheless.

Dry leaves bring him in. I know he is coming, he is not on
    the way
To someplace else, this is no mistake—
Someone is coming to me for love
My limbs are taken apart, my skull is opened out, my chest
    is bared and life thrust in.
There are mounds of dry leaves around my house,
I cannot get myself to burn them.
I slowly drown in the mounds of leaves, I cannot get
    myself to burn them.

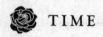 TIME

I no longer care if
I wake at three in the morning.
The day won't bode well
If you do not sleep well
At night—that's what people say.

A day not well spent—who cares anyway!
That day sits away from me, in its own spell,
The night in its broken clock.
My nights awake curl on the feet
Of my sleeping self who cannot find a dream.

All these nights, the terrible times, I have nothing
To do with them. What are you when life and death
Become inseparable?
I cannot slightly lift death out of life
And keep night from day.
There's a sleepwalker in my room
Who rises from this bed, takes shape
In the shattered dark, and paces
Through my house in search of time.

SOIL

The moment I heard you wanted
To give me something, I coiled
Inside myself. Having swam across oceans, I look
For dry wells in which to hide. I am not used
To getting . . . don't give me anything.

When someone who gives puts out
His hands to receive, other hands once used
To receiving perpetually extend, a diamond
Crown on each finger. When you said

'I will give you love,' your face
Turned alien, even your voice
Seemed a calling from some strange planet
I am thrown into, thrust a thousand
Light years away. The leaves on trees, the skin
Of dry rivers, the skies above, all like thin snakes—
No moon or sun—sluice oozing out

From who knows where . . .

Tell me, what do you want?
I'll pawn my life to give it

But do not mention giving. There are some who never get
And not all are used to being given. I feel you salting me
Like a coiling earthworm. You pledged half the sky, but
Save it—take all the love you say you have.
Not all soil is fertile!

A FEW TRANSPARENT YEARS

For some years now, I have been standing
Very close to death. Speechlessly facing
My mother, my father, for a few years now.
I really am not sure if I am alive, for the last few years,
The thin line between being alive and not
Has been reducing to near zero, hanging like a loose thread.

For the last few years, the human that lives inside me,
Has been loathsome, dumb, a tree
That has lost its last October leaf.
Long abandoned by spring, If I die
Today, let me go. Carve an epitaph
Under the branches of this jasmine tree
That is now me, an elegy
I've been writing for the last few years
On a white paper with white ink.

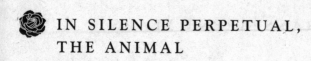

IN SILENCE PERPETUAL,
THE ANIMAL

Today is International Language Day.
I am at home with my cat,
No one else. Nowhere to go.
Today you will sing, today you will dance—

Celebrate language, deck up the city with vowels
And crown yourself with consonants.
Shed tears while reading poetry. Sing along
As you march to the martyr memorial. All flowers
    in the country
Resting there at the foot of the territorial.

Let language be thankful to you.
Today is your day. You, the foot soldiers
Will swear in the name of language
As you prepare for tomorrow. You have to, that's the
    norm for the day.

A day which is not mine . . . though it used to be.
You have driven me away from my language.
You have thrown me off the threshold of words.

I have not uttered another language, not made another
    country my own,
And have waited at your closed doors for ages.
But none dare open. You have seen me

Waiting at the door, but say that you don't see me
As if the country is yours alone,
As if the language is yours alone, the language that I
    speak in
Alone, in the quiet walls where no one can hear.
The language that I write in is not mine.
The language that has reared my infancy, my childhood,
    borne my adolescence,
The language that I dream in, is not mine.
I have loved my language before the city was born—
I dare you to love a single day!

Today is International Language Day,
And I will also celebrate language today in my own way:
I will not utter a word in that language that is yours.
I will not write a single word.
I will celebrate by not dreaming—
I will speak to my cat in the words only we know.

FIRE

1. *Flame*

My room was suddenly on fire yesterday—
A body long cold, deprived of heat and warmth,
An untouched and unfelt cold body—
A fire touched that body yesterday.

An unhindered touch spreads its arms and grows.
Finds the lips on its way.
The raging tongue of fire found its way to the lips
    yesterday, kissed
My chin, my breasts, the curves of my back, my naval and
    my sex.
A fire found its way.

2. *Burn*

The lips wanted to burn away, but they didn't,
The body wanted to burn away, but it didn't.
The little fire could burn nothing of me.

I want to burn myself but not down to ashes.
Why would one want to turn into ashes!

How much can one burn anyway, a lonesome
Person in smouldering in solitude!
This was merely foreplay with fire, nothing
Beyond midnight, quietly finding its way home
At dusk leaving darkness behind.

3. *Coals*

I still do not know if he was the fire or just its nearness.
Maybe he was my warmth, of my own fire!
A body full of fire lying too long in the world's
     mortuary . . .
Maybe it's just me who gradually awoke from the lonely
    slumber.
Maybe it's me who tried to light him up with my own fire,
Maybe it's me who wanted him to smother
The coals, push me under the ground and kick
Leaves over my body. Never. The coals beneath the ash
Are hot—are bold enough to turn the world around.

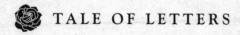

TALE OF LETTERS

The peanut seller comes in the evening . . .
A few lone birds chirp as he comes
Up the stairs to the terrace.
Spices—pepper and coriander leaves—are dried
And curled on the steps.
I am well past the age
To eye roadside Romeos.
Recently I have started to open my door
And wait outside in the mornings.
Not to dry my hair, though.
I have a new affliction of late:

The postman passes in the morning.
Leaves behind a letter, and the kids of the house, unaware, fold
It into paper planes. I stand and wait.

Though it does cross my mind
That you are happily busy with your household—
Happy watering the garden in your yard every afternoon
Happy after an evening out with wife and kids—
Why would you write a letter?
Why will he who is happy write letters
To a woman outside with wet hair, peanut shells?

THRESHOLD, JUST BEFORE MIDNIGHT

I travel enough
But never beyond the threshold.

I keep coming back, in circles
I get stirred—root and branch—in my mind
Everyone arrives except the one that I've longed for all night.

They smile, exchange pleasantries . . .
How much I want to move to a different latitude
Beyond sight, but beyond love too.

I do go, but still, never beyond the threshold.
Blindfolded, he runs around beautiful belles on open grounds.
I want to leave, but someone calls from behind.
Does anyone really call?
In this chamber of echoes, am I calling myself?

SIMILAR DIFFERENCE

They talked about us, and we about them.
There were some we did not serve, and neither did they.

Some were are not ours, not theirs, kin to no one
And some were devoted to their oblivious carnality.

Some have something to talk about, some
Claim to fly with some, or land with some, harbour

Hunger, worms in our innards, decay
In our heaving chests. Some have gangrenous feet—

Malaria, leprosy—some have no ailments in body and
    mind, no
Grief or opulence, some have created rings around
    their fingers,

Have known well the some who walk the fronts and on
    the backs.
We and they have dissociated from some, escaping
    the clutches

Of heavy paws, of yellow cobras. We don't have, they
    don't have
Nothing, no rings, no fingers, no stomach, so

Let there be nothing. Let we and them live happily,
    truthfully.

SO LET THEM RULE THE WORLD!

Let all the doors of the world's arsenals swing open.
Let them wield their swords and hang rifles from
    their waists . . .
Let them clutch grenades in their fists.

And with the grand inspiration of Dār al-Islam in their
    minds
Let them go into the streets and behead the infidel.

After wrapping their obedient heads with veils
And confining them to their rooms, let them torture
Women to death, let the rapists go berserk

Door-to-door and copulate their erect hysteria
And beget male babies in this overcrowded

World. Let all men become Taliban overnight . . .
Let them seize the entire planet
From Argentina to Iceland, from the Maldives to Morocco,
From the Bahamas to Bangladesh—

May the whole universe become their citadel.

Let the leaders of the world bow down
Upon the sacred land of Islam, now everywhere, and let
Their heads be crowned, these terrorists, one by one.

Yes, let the world's leaders apologize with folded hands
For their own cruel misdeeds. Let them together imbibe
The holy water—the *Charanamrita* of these true
    believers—
And be so blessed by their grace, their God, their gravitas.

SELF-PORTRAIT

I don't believe in God.
I look upon nature with wondering eyes.
However much I grasp the hand of progress
    society's hindrances take hold of my sleeve
    and gradually pull me backwards.
I wish I could walk all through the city
    in the middle of the night,
    sitting down anywhere alone to cry.

I don't believe in God.
From house to house the religion-mongers
    secretly divide us into castes,
    segregate the women from the human race.
I, too, am divided—
    defrauded of my human rights.
The crafty politician
    gets loud applause when he rails about class
        exploitation,
But he cleverly suppresses all the explanation
    of women's defamation.
All those people of supposed good character, I know
    them all.

I don't believe in God.
Throughout the world, religion has extended its
    eighteen talons.
      In my lone brandishing, how many of its bones can
        I shatter?
How much can I rip discrimination's far-spreading net?

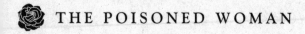

THE POISONED WOMAN

Here are goblets I could choose:
One offers sweetness,
My favourite strawberry juice . . .
Another holds pungent fruit beer.
And I also have the tangy wine
From grapes—yet the goblet
I choose to drink
Always holds poison. The colour of liquor

Always ensnares me. I stare.
That glossy sheen is spellbinding.
So, I drink, and find
Poison turning my throat to fire.

This is where I make myself unwise, choosing
The yellow oleander's toxins
While passing over, unnoticed,
The nectar from hundreds of roses—
Blossom of thorns—petal, stem and root.

A POEM WITH A LOTUS INSIDE

I have written a poem full of the wonders of water,
I have woven words that gift to you a picture
Of a warm red lotus, a water
Lotus, vivid and bright, that I have brought
For him, pulled gently from the water.

Where has he gone?
Who will receive this beautiful blossom,
Who will now read my verse?
He fled like a winter bird on sweeping wings.
Like a sailor, mad for the sea, riding the rising tide.

In my hand, the verse.
In my hand, the water lotus
Droops now. I am left
Longing, feeling like a fool, drowning
In the loneliness of my own dark bloom.

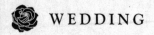

WEDDING

The wedding is in five more days
Sacrificial goat . . . O' girl, you have strayed into a trap!
People all around know you have fallen in love.

In reality, it's death, your death. All your songs will cease!
The lovely picture of life you will hang
On some wall will be bound in a square frame.

New life? Who says it's new?
It's the salt tasted by your mother and grandmother.
But you will taste it now—

When you regret you will only take out handfuls of dream
From the framed life
And put them into your mouth, bitter, in the

Middle of the night. Seeing the frame is dusty, he will snatch
Away your dreams, he, your husband, into whose love you
    have jumped.
Into the well, as everybody does, you have also put your
    neck in a trap,

in full knowledge of things, buried now in brown and
    rocky salt.

 HOOD

O' girl, you start a fire,
O' girl, you flex your golden hood, and hiss—
O' girl, you set everything on fire,
You dance and sing . . .
O' girl, you live.

They are afraid of you.
They are deathly afraid of you, they
Extract your poison, afraid you will flex
Your golden hood. O' girl, keep your poison,
Save your poison, store your poison
A little of the golden poison each and every day.

If you can't throw open the closed window, the shuttered
	door—
If you can't break the chains coiled around your body and
	feet,
Never forget your poison fang, and the death you've saved.

Have you changed anything with your sweet, mellifluous
	speech?
The world has happened without you. Flex the golden hood.

MOTHER'S STORY

1.

Instead of stepping into the darkness, entering
That one silent garden, my mother
Wished to stay and boil Birui rice for me.
She wished to cook fish curry and to fry a whole hilsa.
She wished to mix for me a spicy sauce

With red potatoes, she wished to pick a young coconut
From the south corner of her green, lithe garden.
She wished to fan me with a silken hand fan,
And to remove a few straggly hairs from my forehead.

But my mother's eyes instead became
Yellowish, egg-yoke dead, her belly swelled—
An overly full water tank
Ready to burst. At the end of her days, relatives appeared
Each morning, every evening. 'Be prepared,'
They soothed, 'Be ready to die on the holy day, Friday,
Uttering *la ilaha illallah*, Allah Is One!'

They warned her not to disappoint *Munkar*
And *Nakir*. The relatives wanted

To make certain that her room and yard would be
    clean . . .
That the perfume *shurma* and the blue eyeshadow *atar*
Would be present when Death finally arrived,

And she struggled to breathe,
Her forehead and eyebrows wretched with pain.
The whole house shouted, 'Send your greatest
Respects and reverence to the Prophet!'
No one doubted that she would go to *Jannatul Ferdous*,
To the highest level of heaven. No one doubted

That she would soon walk hand in hand
with Muhammed, a lovely afternoon
In the Garden of Paradise, the silent landscape.
No one doubted that my mother and Muhammed would
Lunch together on pheasant and wine.

My mother then dreamed her lifelong dream:
She would walk with Muhammed
in the Garden of Paradise. She ate the pheasant. She
Drank the dark, dark wine.

But what a surprise! Now, at the very time
She was about to depart this Earth

She hesitated.

She placed a new sheet upon my bed,
And began to sew a frock with colourful embroidery—
Just for me.

Yes, she wished to walk barefoot in her own courtyard,
To prop up a young guava plant with a bamboo stick.
She wished to sing, sitting in the garden of *hasnuhena*,

'Never before had such a bright moon shone down,
Never before was the night so beautiful . . .'

My mother wanted so desperately to live.

2.

There is, I know, no reincarnation,
No last judgment day: heaven, pheasant, wine, pink
    virgins—
Nothing but traps set by true believers.

There is no heaven for Mother to go. She will
Not walk in any dark garden with anyone whatsoever.

Cunning foxes will instead enter her grave, eat
Her flesh—her white bones will be spread by the winds . . .

I do want to believe in Heaven
Over the seventh sky, or somewhere else—
A fabulous, magnificent heaven—
Somewhere my mother would reach
After crossing the *Pulsirat*—
The bridge which seems so impossible.

And there, once she has passed over that bridge
With the greatest of ease,
A very handsome man, the Prophet Muhammed,
Will welcome her, will embrace her.
He will feel her melt upon his broad chest.

She will shower in the glorious fountain.
A pheasant will arrive on a golden tray, and
My mother will eat to her heart's content.
Allah Himself will come by foot into the dark garden
To meet her. He will thread a red flower into her hair,
Kiss her passionately, she will sleep

On a soft feather bed, fanned by seven hundred *Hur*,
    the virgins,
And *gelban* will serve her cool water from a silver pitcher.

145

She will laugh.
Her whole body will shake with enormous happiness.
She will forget her miserable life on Earth . . .

As an atheist, how good I feel—just to imagine—
That somewhere there is really Heaven . . .

GIFT ME YOUR ABSENCE

When I go out for fresh air—
To restaurants, cinemas, theatres,
Concerts or markets, you are nowhere.
When I return home, exhausted, you
Aren't there. You aren't
Next to me in bed.
You are somewhere else.

Maybe you have a new companion now,
Indulging in friendly banter
With an old partner. Still, nowadays
My world is now mine alone.

But my world was once yours too.
When you'd pull my hair or slap me,
I'd think, 'It's his claim to love.'
Taking my life in the palm of your hands,
You spun it like a child's toy, all
In the name of love.
You played with me like a little boy

Whose toy chest is filled to the rim
With flattened wheels from broken, tiny cars.

That day you kicked my back?
Even that day must have been my fault . . .

I made myself miserable over and over again.

The days passed. The moon hung its silver horn.
The sun came out and went again. The wind died down.

And now, I'm no more a puppet in your hands.
I'm not that boy's marble, your spinning top,
Nor am I a kite you can fly.
I'm no more dust or sand,
Nor hay or straw. I'm a whole
Human being, standing up with my spine
Straight. Your absence—the lack and dark of you
Has illuminated my own set of toys, my own
Glorious joy for simply being.
Celebration, meaning, feeling at last
Your absence has taught me to love
Myself. The past? That strange ghost of before? No more.

Diamonds, pearls, red roses—
Not even the utterance of these magical gifts, not
'I love you!'
Will cross the distance between us.
If you really wish to give me something,
Gift me your absence!

THE CYCLE OF LONELINESS

I go to sleep every night with a terrible emptiness within:
When I am about to break, the book
Falls from my hand, the spectacles slip down—
Leaning over my body, gently touching my cheek,
    my emptiness
Runs its fingers through my hair in the dead of night,
    and says,
'You are so tired. Please sleep.'

I sleep, wake up, go to the washroom—the emptiness
    stays along.

At daybreak, the daily rush hour begins, a hundred
People to interact with, I'm running around with the 'Do-
This-and-do-that' . . . my writing, reading, talking, papers
Being found, written, and me always looking for more!
Shopping, eating, daily living—the emptiness stays along
    all through.

The evening at the theatre, fun and frolic; at the
    restaurant, or café,
Greetings and recognitions at all places, houses, even
    sitting happily

On the terrace, gazing at the moon—
Gazing and kissing—
The emptiness stays so close. I go
To sleep, then, just as the night before, and every night,
    with a
Terrible emptiness within:
When I am about to crack, the book
Slips from my hand, the spectacles fall down—
Lying next to my body, softly touching my cheek, the
    emptiness
Slides its fingers through my hair in the quiet of the night,
    and says,
'You are so tired. Please sleep.'

CURSE

I cannot recognize my gait. I do not
Recognize my gaze. Love is breaking me—

My body seems alien, my mind not my own.
The sun and moon? Inconsequential. The spinning world
    and the planets

Crash into satellites, one million pieces of myself.
I cannot recognize myself. I am becoming so strange.

In the company of my friends, when I am supposed
    to laugh,
I do not laugh. When expected to grieve, I giggle.

I cannot lift my mind above love, and for a
    few seconds keep
Still on something else. Darkness keeps the world
    around me

Still. Nowadays, if I have to curse an enemy, I no longer
Say, 'May you be a leper, may you die, you die.'

I can now curse under my breath—*may you fall in love.*

YOU ARE THERE EVEN WHEN YOU ARE NOT

When you're not here with me
You are most with me.
I walk, I feel you walking next to me.

I take you along to the market,
I buy all that you love to eat, knowing well you're not
    around, but
I walk, and feel you walking with me.

I talk to you when you're not with me.
I sit down to eat. I can feel you at the table, too.
When you're not here with me, whatever

I see you also see—
Hear, whatever I hear.
I talk, debate, sing, write poetry, you

Are with me all my waking day, in my dreams
When I sleep . . . you're not here, but your scent upon
The other pillow, the echo of your laugh once here—

When you're not here with me, you're the most with me.

TO ME MY COUNTRY NOW

To me my country is now a crematorium.
A lonely dog stands and whines all night, a few
Pyre-makers lie here and there, drunk to the bone.

My country is no more a vast expanse of
        green croplands—
No more a fast-flowing river, or glittering lake.
No more a grass. No longer a flower nestled among thorns.

My country was my ma's cotton sari end, the end
On which she wiped her sweat and tears and waited
        at the border.
My country was the deep, dark eyes of Ma,
The eyes that bore wings and flew off into both sun and
        nights, would
Find me wherever I floated, drowned, brought me to
        found ground.
My country was my ma's hand-wound hair-bun

Breaking loose, slumped to one side over all my shame.
        My country
Was once puffed rice that Ma mixed with mustard oil,
        fried hilsa

On a cloudy day, my favourite hotchpotch.

My country was the six pairs of bangles on my ma's
    wrist, red
Blue, green, orange, yellow, my country was
My glee of standing in the yard and calling out, 'Ma-Ma!'
Snuggling under her quilt on a chilly winter night—
Sitting on shiuli-strewn grounds with a plateful of
    winter savouries.

Time, the great stealer, packed in darkness afar—
Dug deep under mounds of silence lies
My country, maimed by people who fled
Un-named, there is no one I call my country now. I stand

Among a million pyres, a thirsty dog, and a few
    drunken men.

MISERABLE MA

In an iron chest with termites and
Cockroaches, moth balls, I wished
To stack away my mother's miseries.
On a pleasure trip to the Brahmaputra, no one
      would know
As I let them drift
Like hyacinths, like straw, like dead snakes floating—
My mother's miseries would flow towards Coochbihar.

But the miseries stayed with Ma, went with her to her grave.

I would have taken them to be buried elsewhere, strewn
      them about
Like loose beads from a worn necklace, toss
Them on to railway lines, into the bamboo grove, into
      stinking ponds.
Now I can't! Ma is sleeping, her miseries lie with her, near
      her head
At the dead of night, they whisper to her and her alone.

I once wanted to spray rosewater on to my
      mother's miseries
As if the fragrance would put them all to rest.

In the coal-shed, next to the well or under the tree
    in the yard.
In the evenings, I wanted to lift them lightly up to the terrace
To lose their grief and run around the moon.

It's so hard to live a long, long life. And the miseries
Never left Ma, like too-close relatives, as if
The slightest solitude would trouble her.
Make her slip on muddy grounds. Allow tigers and bears
    to devour her,
To be lifted by *ginns*
On to the top branches of trees . . .

The miseries would talk to Ma in privacy—
Who knows what they chatted about!

The people in her house would offer seats to misery,
A welcome drink, betel leaf and nuts.
One could see the lime on the fingers of those miseries . . .
The miseries would laze around on the beds all afternoon,
Wake up and ask for ablution water before evening prayers.

The prayer mat would be laid out in the middle of the room.
The miseries wrapped up my mother even tighter than
    her clothes.

NO MORE COOKING

You had your family even before your childhood
Passed. You'd sweat and toil from dawn to midnight, cook
Thrice a day, serve all family members, and their guests . . .
Even pour out cool water for them.
As you are swept away in belched sourness,
You are the last to eat.

You and your lonely plate—
The stray alone, the family pet.

Fry the hilsa, singe the mutton well.
What about potato-poppy? Don't forget the mustard.
I hope you have aubergines! Weren't you supposed to stuff
    the gourds?
Don't tell me there's no shrimp! Didn't you say chilli
    chicken?
Don't listen, play deaf.
Let people wait for food,

Move away from those unclean, soiled plates,
Move away, you girl—
Let no more cooking start this very day.

 FLOWER

I kept staring at the jasmine . . . not once did it say that
    you love me.
The white, curled blooms refused to speak, made silent
In the wind between us. If you do love me, if it is love
That you feel for me, whisper in my ear!

If you love me, why doesn't the jasmine know this?
The yellow tendrils dance in the breeze, and so do you—
You could dance such with anyone in your arms behind
    closed doors!
I don't believe you any more. However much you say,
'I'm all yours,' or 'You're the only one,'
Let the birds tell me first, the trees, leaves; let the flower
    say it.
Let the skies say, 'Love'. Make the cloud and rain kiss my
    neck, keep the sun
And moonlight talking, let the neighbours, people on the
    streets and in the markets
Look at us and say, 'Now that is love.' Let the still waters

Of the pond where cold water comes sweet from
    the bucket
Say that you love me! When the words around us

Drive my sinews mad—when your lips confess
    everything had—

I shall, on the crossroads, there in front of one thousand
    thousand men
Kiss you without a care for the world. The day the jasmine

Tells me that you love me, that is when
I shall tell you that I love you too, not a moment before.

AM I NOT TO HAVE A COUNTRY OF MY OWN?

I have raced across the north and the south hemispheres
    like a woman possessed.
Across mountains, and rows of trees through the sky's
    moon mist
And sun, like a blind madwoman desperate for
    destination.
Sifting through the grass, the thorned vines, barren
    grounds and faceless
Humans, I am looking for a nation.
I am such a criminal, an enemy of humanity,
Such a traitor, that I am not to have a country of my own!
Nation wills my nation from the rest of my sightless life.

Once through the world and through with life, if
You pull away from the beaches of the country the thirsty,
    weary man's peace
And cast away the little water I hold in the cup of my
    hands only
To condemn me to death, what name should I call you by,
    my country?

You have stood on my chest like a mountain and pressed

Your boots down upon my neck, gouged out my eyes,
Pulled out my tongue and cut it to pieces. You've flogged

My skin to gorgeous shreds, crushed my legs
And cut open my skull to smash my brains.
Nation, you have held me captive, hoping I would die.
But it is you who I call my country. A love that runs
	too deep

Cannot make a few truths on my lips say 'traitor' in
	your mouth.
Your will to walk shoulder-to-shoulder in liar rallies cannot
Bury my humanity under the earth or throw it to the wind
	in the vast bright sky.
You, my country, have dug out my nation from my life and
	the citizen from my heart.

A LETTER TO MY MOTHER

I am not generous like you, I am not a human like you.
And how many days, many thousands of days, I don't see
    you, Ma?
Many thousands of days, I don't hear your voice.
Many thousands of days, I don't feel your touch.

You brought forth all my wishes, but remained
In the shadows. I took all the pleasures for myself.
No one gave you anything, no one loved you, not
    even me.

You were here, but never knew you were here.
Like magic, you filled my needs—
When I got hungry, when I was thirsty,
When I wanted to play, when my heart opened, when my
    heart closed—
You knew before I knew.

Did I ever love you back? Did I give you something
    human?

The cleaner, the cook, the one behind the smoke.
You alone carried all your pain, you cried alone.

No one was there for you, no one held you, lifted you
    up . . . not even me.

You cured other's diseases like a magician.
No one cured you, not even me.

I killed you before you knew that I was killing you.
You are not here, and suddenly I feel through my spine
And inside my veins, that you are not here.
My pride is barred under the stone of your absence.
I want to bear that same pain you once bore.
I can't, I could not, I am no magician—
Not even some cheap trickster of life.

DEPARTURE, DEPARTURE

This is exactly how, slowly, in unfaltering steps, you will
leave one day.

One day you will not turn back.

There is a gaze fixed on the path you will leave by.

You will simply say so and move away like a sharpened knife.

You will not utter a word about ever meeting again.

I won't heave a sigh for you having left.

If you look back, you will see me looking away.

My eyes are made of stone. My face a piece of plank.

I knew you would leave thus, setting ablaze a farm-full
dream of the harvest.

I will let it burn, make no attempts to bring salvage.

I clean the gravel on the way and lay out a red carpet for
those who wish to leave.

A PASSION FOR SOLITUDE

I live alone—some people
Think I suffer from loneliness!

They think I must be up all night
Staring helplessly at those wooden ceiling beams, as if
    I stumble
Upon the road every now and then when walking;
As if a herd of wild buffalo
Is forever chasing me, as if

A shiver of sharks will attack me
If I set a single foot in public water!
How do I make them understand?

I live alone—the way I wish to live.
If my house is ever overcrowded, I feel glum.
When people's eyes follow me, I stand
There feeling awkward, embarrassed.
My days and nights fall flat and lay
Face downwards, on the entrance of my porch . . .

I feel the loneliest when I'm not alone any more.
When my well-wishers sit on my lap—

When a friend stands too close to me,
When those who love me fall over my head
In a bid to express their love—
I need to breathe, dodge the big stones
Thrown down those alleys of my thoughts as they bite
Huge chunks from my true self, and sniff at my
   public blood.

SURELY ONE DAY

There will come a day— I'll wait for you, you'll return home,
I'll prepare tea for you.
A clean towel for you in the shower,
And clothes to wear after; I'll hand
You your pair of slippers to wear!
If you put the toilet seat up, I'll put it down.
If you forget to flush, I'll flush it for you.
I'll spread your favourite dishes on the dining table.
As you approach the last bite of one thing I'll
Keep putting more on your plate, from shukto to sandesh.
The more you eat, the happier I'll be!

There will come a day when, having food, you'll share
With me your whereabouts for the day
And I'll feel so blessed and gratified!
You're thinking of me as your own
Surely because you love me!
When you caress me, loving my body
And no else's, I become dizzy
Only because you love only me.

If you run a fever, there will come a day
I'll become the world's best nurse.

I'll call the doctor, stay
Awake all night pressing damp washcloths to your
    forehead.
I will sponge your body, give
You each pill exactly on time.
There will come a day that I run a fever. You'll say,
'The season's changing.'
If I have a cough, you'll say,
'An allergy for sure . . . go take your pills.'
If I have a stomach ache, you'll say,
'What kind of junk have you been eating?'
If I have a backache, you'll say,
'How can you be so old so young?'
If I have knee pain, you'll say,
'You've become a storehouse
Of illnesses,' if I have a headache, you'll say,
'It's nothing; you'll be fine in no time.'
If you find a few grey strands on my head, you'll say,
'Tell me how old you *really* are?'

There will come a day I'll wish
To visit the mountains—you'll say
'I don't have the time to go.'
'I have enough time . . . can I go then?' I'll ask.
'You wish to go alone?'
I'll laugh and say, 'Yes, I'll go alone!'

Hearing me, you'll laugh out so loud and say,
'Are you insane? Who'll take care of me then?
Who'll cook for me? Who'll serve me food?
Who'll wash all my clothes? Who'll arrange them?
Who'll clean my house and bed?
Who'll guard the house?
Who'll water the garden?'
I'll answer, 'You.'

That will be a day when you'll roll
Your eyes in surprise! I'll correct myself and say,
'Your maid will do it for you.'
You'll say, 'I don't like the food she cooks,
The way you take care of everything as your own,
The maid doesn't do it.'
I'll laugh. My heart
Will overflow with a fountain of joy:
If my culinary skills are better than the maid's
Then I'm not your maid. I'm different.
My heart will skip a beat in joy:
Your world isn't the maid's, it's mine!

There will come a day—suitcase packed
To visit the ocean alone—and you will
Pounce on me, hyena on a deer.
You'll tear me up, make me bleed.

169

Seeing my wounds, my near and dear
Ones will say, 'Oh! It isn't blood,
But only a sign of his love for you.
He acts this way only because he loves you,
He can't live without you even for short while.'
And so you want me! I'll wipe
My tears and smile again, enter
The kitchen to prepare your favourite sweet dish rasmalai
    for you!

But there will come a day
When I won't prepare tea for you any more.
I will not hand you your pair of slippers.
I won't flush the toilet for you,
I won't prepare that favourite dish,
One of these days I'll stop staying up all night.
If you run a fever,
Keeping a vigilant eye on the watch
I'll spend that day in the hills if I feel like,
And bathe in the ocean if I wish to!

FORGETFUL

There's so much I shouldn't forget, yet I do!
I shouldn't forget the day I was crowned,
The day I graduated from college.

The day I swam across a shallow river.
The day I escaped alive from the hyena's cave,
The day I first opened my eyes

After being in a coma for a good three months.
The day I carried out a procession, tearing
Apart the throne of a tyrannical ruler—

I shouldn't forget any of these, yet I do!

But I'll never forget when and where I first met you.
The day you first touched my hands,
The day I first knew you loved me . . .

The day you denied me and walked your way to fame.
I shouldn't remember you, yet I do! The more
I think of forgetting you, the more I remember:

No matter how many times I tell the neighbours,

You're worthless, you're a stone, no matter
How much I wish to forget you, secretly

I know I don't wish to forget you.

If I do, how will I touch my own hands?
By becoming you when it's dark?
If I do, how will I love myself
The way I do love, by being you!

THE WRONG PERSON

Let's work to search for the wrong person—
Have a heart-to-heart with them,
And exchange love.

Mistakes are the only things that remain.
The excitement of not knowing a mistake—
Or coming apart at its sudden discovery, or falling
In love with a mistake—whatever is left of life, let it pass as

I search for the wrong person, if I search at all.

Life now is about enduring,
About weeding out all the dreams
And nursing the poison trees.
Watching the mournful sun set through someone else's
    eyes,
Singing someone else's song, to someone else's tune,
    and suffering.

I once sought out that someone who would make
This life worthwhile, or this sky worthwhile—but
It's always been someone else I face,

It's always been someone else who's touched me,
Someone else who clouds over my days.

Now I can play house with a mistake consciously.
Now I can roam the hills with them, too.
I can trade in one mistake for another, wade

Into its dangerous depth sans worry, without doubt or
    apprehension.
I can get close to my mistake knowing fully well that it is
    just that.

CORONA HAD ONCE KISSED ME

1.

The little girl Corona entered my house one day . . .
I don't know how!
I tried so hard to lock and bolt my door,
I tried so hard to block the sky and the air.
I sat holding my breath so she
Wouldn't see a single strand of my hair,
Nor an eyelash, or even a toenail.
Yet, she did see me!
She did come and pounce at my body,
She'd kiss my lips, she sat touching my
Tongue with hers. The more
I tried pulling her down,
The tighter she hugged me.
She slithered on her chest like a snake,
Entering my sanctum secretly—alone!

Corona loves playing a game of war—
And war the whole night.
And she loves playing the same game
Of war the whole day. It's exhausting!

2.

Corona hoists her victory flag
On the roof of my house!

My room and balcony,
My bed and pillow,
My writing table,
Corona owns them all.
My rice and pulses,
My fruits and vegetables,
My eggs and milk . . .

Everything's in her control.
The girl took over my world,
Sold all my books, whatever was mine, she took it all.
She even made my cat sit in the corner!
But now? The cat seeks her out!

The girl named Corona is dancing
in the absolute madness of my body
As if she's the unchallenged queen
of the universe. Yet rapt in her joyous ecstasy
She has carelessly stepped on my throat—
Oh! I'm choking on Corona's
Desperate hunger, she's tearing away

And eating up my heart, my lungs . . .
She's clawing out my eyes, eating
My very flesh and throwing away my bones,
Sucking up my brain in a single sip.

3.

Oh, Corona, you came with a smiling face and kissed me.
Lovingly, you came to live with me
In my entire body. You don't know
You're incapable of living, Corona, you
Don't know people call you death.

The young girl had come to town
Tinkling her anklet, the anklet
Of death she wore in her ankles.

4.

Bitten by this young little girl,
So many have been thrown away
Like black ants with the garbage.
Those who stood still turned all blue

As if they'd drunk poison . . . don't they remember, while
Kissing her they'd sucked the young girl's saliva?

Corona is nobody to me, yet
She invites me closer to her time and again.
Yet, she comes silently, making
No sound she comes in the middle
Of the night, she comes while the whole city sleeps . . .
She comes to see how much of me is left.

SHACKLE

There's a death lying over my long body;
A death breathing over me, I can hear it.
A death fast asleep, waking up from its slumber
And ransacking my garden, I can hear it.
It's burning all my roses, I can feel the heat.

Suddenly in the middle of the night or mid-afternoon,
Hearing the footsteps of a nightmare in my slumber,
My heart jolts and I wake to find
I'm not breathing any more.
There's no vibration in my lungs,
My hands and legs aren't moving either.
My heart has stopped beating.
The pupils of my eyes are dead and wide!

I'm not breathing, death is.
Death is living in my long body,
Is growing up and growing taller—
It has almost reached my height!
In the mirror I see death's eye across from mine.
One day I discovered with these wondrous eyes
That this death had grown taller than my tall body . . .

It has now almost fully traded my one life
For the death that will become fiercely alive, and inside
Some bleak corner of that death I'll be crouching,
Holding the shell of life in my hands.
Death will mistakenly address me.
I'll want to respond,
But my throat will have no voice.
I'll want to run away,
But my feet will be tied with a strong, strong shackle.

UPSET

All wharfs don't work for me.
I can't deal with any and every love,
I can't be with any and every man. You see,
I was upset when I said I don't want
To see you any more; when I said, 'I don't love you'
You heard my words and hid from my eyes . . .

Now you anchor your boat
Wherever you wish.

Any and every love works for you!

My anger has faded,
Yet, I'm not calling you back.
I understand well you don't think
Of me or love me any more.
But see, I'm not anchoring my boat
in every quay like you. There's a
Following sea at my keel. A lovely
Wind carries me along on one tall wave.

I don't write poetry, I write life on paper.
I don't write poems; the wind that hits my body
When I stand on the top of a hill? I pen it down.

But I do write about love too!
I do it very secretly, though . . .

Sitting next to the black ocean in a deep, dark night,
I hear the lamenting sound of the waves in tears and
I pen it down. I go close to the river and write

About the chaos and noise the fishes, the kingfishers and
Human beings make. I'm not a poet, only a thirsty
Wanderer. I keep globetrotting, and note
The hissing sound of hatred . . .
I pen down wars.
I smell the stench emanating from
Piles of corpses and write about it.
When I see people busy killing people,

I write about it, I note it down.
If I don't find a pen or ink,
I write with the blood of my fingers . . .

Yet always, I keep writing, until
There's a way, I'll point at the thorns in the way.
I'll pen down the sorrow and pain,
I'll write about the wails and laments
Of people's unrestrained jealousy and anger.
I'll write about the fire burning the forests,

And bring more light to the huffing of
Scared little sparrows, cheetahs and chital deer,
Running here and there to save their innocent lives.
Then, when all game ends, when all fall asleep in their
    cosy beds,
I'll sit down to write about love!

ACKNOWLEDGEMENTS

Many people put forth tremendous effort to make this book happen. First and foremost, I am grateful for the artistic grace and power—and wonderful friendship—formed and nurtured by Taslima Nasrin herself. Her presence in our communities and cultures is simply priceless, and I'm so proud and lucky to have known her for all these years. Samik Bandapadyay, Samik Roy, Niharika Mishra, Sreejita Basu, Warren Allen Smith, Aarohi Bhattacharya and Maharghya Chakraborty were instrumental in first moving these poems into the English language, and the late Carolyn Wright must be given great credit for her work translating Ms Nasrin's collection *The Game in Reverse*; I have approached some of these poems and re-translated them here in this current collection.

Many thanks to Hall Gardner for working on the initial translations of some of these poems, and I'm immensely appreciative of and humbled by the work of Chirag Thakkar and his team at Penguin for believing in this collection and understanding the importance of bringing these poems into a global readership. And last but not least, I could not have completed this collection without the love and support of Alyson Zerbe and Bleys Waters, my lifelong companions.